T&T CLARK STUDY GUIDES TO THE OLD TESTAMENT

Isaiah: A Paradigmatic Prophet and His Interpreters

Series Editor
Adrian Curtis, University of Manchester, UK
Published in association with the Society for Old Testament Study

T0353232

Other titles in the series include:

Amos: An Introduction and Study Guide

1 & 2 Kings: An Introduction and Study Guide

1 & 2 Samuel: An Introduction and Study Guide

Ecclesiastes: An Introduction and Study Guide

Exodus: An Introduction and Study Guide

Ezra-Nehemiah: An Introduction and Study Guide

Haggai, Zechariah, and Malachi: An Introduction and Study Guide

Hebrews: An Introduction and Study Guide

Lamentations: An Introduction and Study Guide

Leviticus: An Introduction and Study Guide

Jeremiah: An Introduction and Study Guide

Job: An Introduction and Study Guide

Joel, Obadiah, Habakkuk, Zephaniah: An Introduction and Study Guide

Joshua: An Introduction and Study Guide

Psalms: An Introduction and Study Guide

Song of Songs: An Introduction and Study Guide

Numbers: An Introduction and Study Guide

T&T CLARK STUDY GUIDES TO THE NEW TESTAMENT

1 & 2 Thessalonians: An Introduction and Study Guide

1 Peter: An Introduction and Study Guide

2 Corinthians: An Introduction and Study Guide

Colossians: An Introduction and Study Guide

Ephesians: An Introduction and Study Guide

Galatians: An Introduction and Study Guide

James: An Introduction and Study Guide

John: An Introduction and Study Guide

Luke: An Introduction and Study Guide

Mark: An Introduction and Study Guide

Matthew: An Introduction and Study Guide

Philemon: An Introduction and Study Guide

Philippians: An Introduction and Study Guide
Romans: An Introduction and Study Guide
The Acts of the Apostles: An Introduction and Study Guide
The Letters of Jude and Second Peter: An Introduction and Study Guide

Isaiah: A Paradigmatic Prophet and His Interpreters

An Introduction and Study Guide

C. L. Crouch and Christopher B. Hays

t&tclark

LONDON • NEW YORK • OXFORD • NEW DELHI • SYDNEY

T&T CLARK
Bloomsbury Publishing Plc
50 Bedford Square, London, WC1B 3DP, UK
1385 Broadway, New York, NY 10018, USA
29 Earlsfort Terrace, Dublin 2, Ireland

BLOOMSBURY, T&T CLARK and the T&T Clark logo are
trademarks of Bloomsbury Publishing Plc

First published in Great Britain 2022

For legal purposes the Acknowledgements on p. xiii constitute an
extension of this copyright page.

Cover design by clareturner.co.uk

Bloomsbury Publishing Plc does not have any control over, or responsibility for, any third-party
websites referred to or in this book. All internet addresses given in this book were correct
at the time of going to press. The author and publisher regret any inconvenience caused if
addresses have changed or sites have ceased to exist, but can accept no responsibility for any
such changes.

A catalogue record for this book is available from the British Library.

Library of Congress Cataloging-in-Publication Data
Names: Crouch, Carly L. (Carly Lorraine), 1982- author. |
Hays, Christopher B., 1973- author.
Title: Isaiah : an introduction and study guide / by C.L. Crouch
and Christopher B. Hays.
Description: London ; New York : T&T CLARK, 2022. |
Series: T&T Clark's study guides to the Old Testament |
Includes bibliographical references and index. |
Summary: "Introduces the Book of Isaiah, examining its characteristics,
historical context, and theological messaging, as well as the reception history of Isaiah
and what the text has meant to people across history"– Provided by publisher.
Identifiers: LCCN 2022009923 (print) | LCCN 2022009924 (ebook) |
ISBN 9780567680341 (paperback) | ISBN 9780567693761 (hardback) |
ISBN 9780567680358 (pdf) | ISBN 9780567680365 (epub)
Subjects: LCSH: Bible. Isaiah–Study and teaching. |
Bible. Isaiah–Criticism, interpretation, etc.
Classification: LCC BS1515.55 .C76 2022 (print) |
LCC BS1515.55 (ebook) | DDC 224/.106–dc23/eng/20220309
LC record available at https://lccn.loc.gov/2022009923
LC ebook record available at https://lccn.loc.gov/2022009924

ISBN: HB: 978-0-5676-9376-1
          PB: 978-0-5676-8034-1
          ePDF: 978-0-5676-8035-8
          ePUB: 978-0-5676-8036-5

Series: T&T Clark Study Guides to the Old Testament

Typeset by Integra Software Services Pvt. Ltd.

To find out more about our authors and books visit www.bloomsbury.com
and sign up for our newsletters.

To the memory of
Hans Magnus Barstad (1947–2020)
Formidable scholar, generous mentor, and beloved member of the
Society for Old Testament Study

Contents

4   Isaiah in the fifth century 85

Series preface

How can a potential reader be sure that a Guide to a biblical book is balanced and reliable? One answer is 'If the Guide has been produced under the auspices of an organisation such as the Society for Old Testament Study.'

Founded in 1917, the Society for Old Testament Study (or SOTS as it is commonly known) is a British and Irish society for Old Testament scholars, but with a world-wide membership. It seeks to foster the academic study of the Old Testament/Hebrew Bible in various ways, for example by arranging Conferences (usually twice per year) for its members, maintaining links with other learned societies with similar interests in the British Isles and abroad, and producing a range of publications, including scholarly monographs, and collections of essays by individual authors or on specific topics. Periodically it has published volumes seeking to provide an overview of recent developments and emphases in the discipline at the time of publication. The annual Society for Old Testament Study Book List, containing succinct reviews by members of the Society of works on the Old Testament and related areas which have been published in the previous year or so, has proved an invaluable bibliographical resource.

With the needs of students in particular in mind, the Society also produced a series of Study Guides to the books of the Old Testament. This first series of Old Testament Guides, published for the Society by Sheffield Academic Press in the 1980s and 1990s, under the general editorship of the late Professor Norman Whybray, was well received as a very useful resource which teachers could recommend to their students with confidence. But it has inevitably become dated with the passage of time, hence the decision that a new series should be commissioned.

The aim of the new series is to continue the tradition established by the first Series, namely to provide a concise, comprehensive, manageable and affordable guide to each biblical book. The intention is that each volume will contain an authoritative overview of the current thinking on the traditional matters of Old Testament/Hebrew Bible introduction, addressing matters of content, major critical issues, and theological perspectives, in the light of recent scholarship, and suggesting suitable further reading. Where appropriate to the particular biblical book or books, attention may also be given to less traditional approaches or particular theoretical perspectives.

All the authors are members of the Society, known for their scholarship and with wide experience of teaching in Universities and Colleges. The series general editor, Adrian Curtis, taught Old Testament/Hebrew Bible at the University of Manchester for many years, is a former Secretary of the Society, and was President of the Society for 2016.

It is the hope of the Society that these Guides will stimulate in their readers an appreciation of the body of literature whose study is at the heart of all its activities.

Acknowledgements

Parts of the chapter on Isaiah of Jerusalem appeared previously in Christopher B. Hays and C. L. Crouch, 'The Historical Context of First Isaiah', in *The Oxford Handbook to Isaiah*, ed. Lena-Sofia Tiemeyer (Oxford: Oxford University Press, 2020), 145–58. Parts of the chapter on Third Isaiah appeared previously in C. L. Crouch, 'Isaiah 56–66', *Guidelines* 36 (2021): 72–94. Material elsewhere also draws on Christopher B. Hays, 'Isaiah', in *The Oxford Encyclopedia of the Books of the Bible*, ed. Michael D. Coogan (Oxford: Oxford University Press, 2011), 1:384–409. We are grateful to Oxford University Press and the Bible Reading Fellowship for their permission to draw on these materials.

*

Biblical translations are taken from the NRSV, with a few minor adjustments for clarity, some of which are indicated. One systematic adaptation has been to render the divine name with its Hebrew consonants ('Yhwh') rather than 'the Lord', since the present purpose is scholarly rather than liturgical.

Introduction

The book of Isaiah is one of the most celebrated and influential literary works of antiquity. Isaiah is first among the Hebrew prophets, and not only in canonical order. The eighth-century prophet's messages and the way they were adapted and shaped by later authors were deeply formative for those who came after him, both within the book of Isaiah and beyond it.

The book's influence is already felt in other books of the Hebrew Bible. The books of Jeremiah and Isaiah share oracular material concerning the nation of Moab (Isa 15–16; Jer 48), and Jeremiah may at one time have been organized to mirror Isaiah's structure of hope after judgement. Isaiah and Ezekiel debate the presence of foreigners in the temple (Isa 56; Ezek 44), even as the latter concurs with Isaiah's emphasis on the profound moral significance of the divine holiness. The influence of Isaiah is also discernible in the Book of the Twelve (the twelve shorter prophetic books also known as the Minor Prophets). Isaiah and the Book of the Twelve span the same period of time; the two collections seem to have been formed concurrently, and their editing was probably carried out by the same scribes. More specifically, the book of Micah can be viewed as a version of Isaiah in miniature – indeed, a Masoretic scribal note on Mic 3:12 observes that the shift from judgement to blessing (in Mic 4:1) is the midpoint of the Book of the Twelve, mirroring the analogous shift to a more positive outlook at Isa 40. The famous oracle about beating swords into ploughshares appears in both books (Isa 2:4; Mic 4:3).

For the subsequent two millennia, the book has continued to shape the thinking of whole religions and nations. The book was prominent among the Roman-period Qumran community associated with the Dead Sea Scrolls: fragments from twenty-one distinct Isaiah scrolls have been found at the site (more than any other biblical book besides Psalms and Deuteronomy) and Isaiah is quoted in numerous sectarian compositions. In rabbinic Jewish tradition, half of the *haftaroth* (selections from the prophets for reading in the synagogue) are drawn from Isaiah – including ten chosen for the Shabbats around Tisha b'Av, when Jews mourn the destruction of the temple. The book's promises of restoration have also played a significant role in the modern Zionist movement; the Eretz Israel museum in Tel Aviv, for example, displays Isa 35:1 prominently, as it invokes the reference to 35:10: 'The ransomed of the Lord shall return, and come to Zion with singing.' The book's reception in Christian tradition has also been extraordinarily rich; John 12:41 reports that 'Isaiah saw [Jesus'] glory and spoke about him' and the prophet was deemed a 'fifth evangelist' already by early Christian interpreters. The book also speaks to those without a religious connection to it; the swords-into-ploughshares passage, for example, is taken up repeatedly in art surrounding the United Nations headquarters in New York.

Isaiah is also one of the most complex and challenging ancient texts to read. This difficulty is multifaceted. Any ancient text comes out of cultural contexts that are lost to many contemporary readers. In Isaiah's case, the book's composition spanned several centuries, which means that the reader needs to know something about a wide span of history in order to appreciate its authors' messages. Isaiah was also written in ancient cities like Jerusalem and (perhaps) Babylon that were crossroads of international influences, which means that some awareness of the wider ancient world is also advisable. Last but not least, very few readers come to the book free of the weight of centuries of interpretation – in synagogue, church, and beyond. Our perceptions of the book are coloured by what we know it *must* say, because we have been told that it does.

The goals of this study guide are to bring into focus some of the major themes and emphases of the book and its parts; to illuminate some of its perplexities with reference to information about its contexts; to explain the processes by which it came to have its present form; and to nod where possible to the ways it has been received in more recent times. It is a brief work, and as such only a starting point. Each section is followed by suggestions for further reading – each of which is itself only a starting point. The book of Isaiah opens out onto a vast panorama; this volume offers a small window into its world.

Formation of the book

The idea that the book of Isaiah was composed in different periods by different authors is one of the most widely accepted conclusions in all of biblical scholarship. Since the nineteenth century and the work of Bernhard

Duhm – who was developing observations made at least as early as the Jewish exegete Abraham Ibn Ezra in the twelfth century CE – the book has been divided into three sections. The first comprises texts appropriate to the eighth century BCE, during the monarchic period of ancient Judah. These are attributed to Isaiah ben ('son of') Amoz, also known as Isaiah of Jerusalem. The second section contains material related to the sixth-century exilic period, which is attributed to an anonymous prophet of that time. The third is made up of texts that reflect a still later period in the development of these ideas, and are attributed to a post-exilic prophet or editor. These historically discrete sections of the book are often referred to as First Isaiah (Isa 1–39), Second Isaiah (or 'Deutero-Isaiah,' Isa 40–55) and Third Isaiah (or 'Trito-Isaiah,' Isa 56–66).

Passages that exhibit a clear interest in the politics of the eighth century, like Isa 8, are associated with Isaiah ben Amoz in Jerusalem. Such passages are concerned with announcing God's coming judgement on the nation of Judah. They emphasize YHWH's sovereignty and holiness and are interested in the implications of these aspects of the divine character for the people's behaviour.

The book skips over the Babylonian exile, although various parts of it look forward to it (e.g. Isa 39) or back at it (e.g. Isa 40:1–2).

Differences in tone and historical backdrop are among the most important reasons that the final twenty-seven chapters of the book, in their entirety, are viewed as originating later than the eighth-century prophet whose name the book bears. Passages such as Isa 45 refer explicitly to the sixth-century Persian king Cyrus, whose defeat of Babylon resulted in the eventual return of some of the deportees and their descendants to Judah, as well as the rebuilding of the Temple (Ezra 1). Isaiah 40–55 and other, related material are designed to reassure the people that God has not forgotten them but will save them from their current plight. This hopeful material makes most sense as the work of an anonymous prophet active in the sixth century. As in First Isaiah, there is a strong emphasis on the kingship of YHWH in these chapters.

Not all of the visions of Jerusalem's restoration imagined by these passages came to pass, however, and a third section of the book tries to explain why this was the case. These latest additions to the book, gathered together in Isa 56–66, attribute the delay in fulfilment to the misbehaviour of the returnees. The people's failure to recognize YHWH as the one true God, creator of the entire universe, together with their unwillingness to act according to principles of divine justice, are especially prominent concerns.

Although this threefold scheme is a highly useful, heuristic way of talking about the book and its development, it turns out to be not too complicated, but rather too simple. Most notably, there is postexilic material in 'First Isaiah', as well as multiple historical layers within Isa 40–55 and Isa 56–66. Furthermore, recent scholars have identified a significant stage in the book's development in the late seventh century, in connection with the decline of Assyrian imperial power and hopes for Judah's renewed independence.

Taking this into account, the developing book of Isaiah appears to have undergone an episode of major revision about every other generation, beginning in the late eighth century with the prophetic activity of Isaiah ben Amoz and continuing through the middle of the fifth century, around the time of Ezra and Nehemiah. The following pages trace the book of Isaiah through each of these major stages, exploring the way it inspired interpretation and reinterpretation, so that its final form serves as a repository of prophetic reflection over the course of nearly three centuries.

Before turning to this tour of Isaiah through the centuries, it is useful to introduce some of the wider issues relating to prophetic activity and prophetic literature, in order to contextualize the historical and literary phenomena reflected in its pages.

Prophetic activity

A prophet is someone who acts as an intermediary between the divine and human worlds. In the biblical tradition, prophets are presented as a key locus of communication with YHWH, responsible for conveying messages from YHWH to the people and from the people to YHWH. Prophets conveyed messages of the people's distress and lamentation to YHWH, and some of them interceded with YHWH on the people's behalf, asking YHWH to relent concerning punishment (Num 14:11–19; Amos 7:1–6; Isa 6:11; Jer 7:16; 11:14; 14:11; cf. Jer 42:2–4).

But most of the activity that the biblical traditions describe prophets engaged in concerns communication in the other direction: conveying messages from YHWH to the people. Frequently these comprise complaints about the people's tendency to worship other deities instead of or alongside YHWH; this is interpreted as a sign of their disloyalty to YHWH. Closely related to this are prophetic admonishments regarding the kind of behaviour appropriate to those who profess to follow the way of YHWH, which the people are said not to be adequately engaged in.

Other prophetic figures in the ancient Near East have a similar function, conveying messages back and forth between heaven and earth. Indeed, it is useful to understand ancient Near Eastern prophetic phenomena as part of a wider category of activities designed to help human beings and their gods communicate. Scholars use the word 'divination' to describe this general category. A prophet is thus a type of 'diviner': a person in a society who has a special role in helping fellow human beings understand the will of the gods.

The wider category of divination includes many different ways in which a person might perceive a message from a god. These may be divided into two major types: technical divination, which requires special training, and intuitive divination, which relies on divine messages that are more or less comprehensible without special training. Technical divination includes activities like interpreting cloud formations, interpreting marks on animal entrails, and interpreting dregs in the bottom of wine goblets. One of the most common forms of divination, especially in Mesopotamia, was extispicy: the examination of the entrails of sacrificed animals for irregularities that might be revelatory. Babylonian astronomy and astrology were also internationally famous, though these efforts to discern the will of the gods by consulting the heavenly bodies are mocked in Second Isaiah (Isa 47:12–13).

The idea behind these technical forms of divination was that the gods could communicate their wishes by manipulating various natural phenomena, such as the marks on a sacrificed animal's liver or the formations of oil on water. The role of the technical diviner was to use the detailed knowledge of these signs and their meaning in order to understand the will of the gods, and then to convey that information to their fellow human beings so they could adapt their behaviour accordingly.

Most of these techniques are viewed with great suspicion in the modern West, influenced in no small way by the biblical rejection of many of them. Yet the biblical texts also attest to the use of a wide variety of divinatory techniques in ancient Israel and Judah. King Saul asks for Samuel to be summoned back from the dead, and the woman he consults on the matter is shown as successfully doing so (1 Sam 28:6–25). Consultation of the dead appears also in Isaiah, where it is more overtly rejected, apparently on the basis that the spirits consulted are those of deceased ancestors, rather than Yhwh (Isa 8:19–22). Joseph is depicted as having prophetic dreams himself, as well as interpreting the dreams of pharaoh and his servants (Gen 37; 40–41). The legends of Daniel also cast him as an interpreter of the divine will by means of royal dreams (Dan 2; 4) as well as his own dreams and visions (Dan 4; 7–12). Daniel also interprets mysterious writings that are unintelligible to others (Dan 5). Prophets are closely associated with 'dreamers of dreams' by Deuteronomy, which is concerned that diviners of either sort might lead the people away from the appropriate worship of Yhwh (Deut 13:1–5). The priestly Urim and Thummim were used for the discernment of Yhwh's will by casting dice or lots (e.g. Exod 38:30; 1 Sam 14:41).

Thus, although Yahwists in ancient Israel and Judah did exclude and condemn some divination practices from the wider ancient Near Eastern repertoire, they also made use of many of them. When Isaiah ben Amoz told King Ahaz to ask for a sign (Isa 7:11), part of Ahaz's hesitation may well have come from his uncertainty as to what kind of sign he should choose. Spoken (and then written) prophecy eventually became the dominant form of divination in ancient Israel, but the biblical texts make clear that there was more religious diversity in the background than the canonical emphasis on prophecy might at first suggest.

Prophecy, as a means of conveying the will of the deity to the people, is considered a form of 'intuitive' divination: for the most part, a prophet did not require extensive specialized training with liver models showing different kinds of markings, or a reference library of celestial omens (for example), in order to interpret the deity's messages. Prophetic communication occurs mostly in words – which, while not necessarily self-explanatory, are at least comprehensible. The use of visual images, as when Amos sees a symbolic basket of summer fruit and other items (Amos 8), or prophetic sign-acts, in which the prophet conveys a message through symbolic actions, as when Isaiah walks around Jerusalem naked to signify the defeat and humiliation of the Egyptians (Isa 20), are usually either fairly straightforward or are accompanied by a verbal explanation.

But spoken prophecy was not unique to ancient Israel and Judah, either; it was common throughout the ancient Near East (Nissinen). An inscription discovered at Deir 'Alla, in modern Jordan, describes a vision of a 'seer' (*ḥzh*) called Balaam, using terminology familiar from biblical literature. Isaiah, Amos, Micah, Ezekiel, Habakkuk and Daniel are all said to 'see' (*ḥzh*) Yhwh's messages concerning Judah and Israel (Isa 1:1; 2:1; 13:1; Ezek 12:27; Amos 1:1; Mic 1:1; Hab 1:1; Dan 4:10; 7:1) and 'seer' or 'visionary' appears to have been common terminology for prophets during certain parts of Israel's and Judah's history, in keeping with similar terminology elsewhere (1 Sam 9; 2 Sam 24:11; 2 Kgs 17:13; Isa 30:10; Amos 7:12; 1 Chr 29:29; 2 Chr 9:29; 19:2).

There are also a number of short prophetic oracle collections preserved from the royal libraries of Assyria, mostly concerning the security of the king and his rule. Narrative accounts from Mesopotamia and Anatolia further record the conveyance of significant prophetic words from local contexts to the royal court, where their veracity could be investigated via technical divination. Notably, a number of these ancient Near Eastern traditions attest to prophetic (and other divinatory) activity by women. Although the surviving prophetic literature of ancient Israel and Judah is all attributed to male prophets, several women in the Hebrew Bible are identified as prophets (nᵉbîʾah, the feminine form of the common noun nabî, 'prophet'; e.g. Exod 15:20, Judg 4:4; Isa 8:3; Neh 6:14) or are described as prophesying (e.g. Huldah in 2 Kgs 22:14–20; Stökl and Carvalho).

The ancient Near Eastern references to prophetic activity affirm the impression gained from the biblical material regarding diviners' and prophets' social role, namely, that they did not speak abstractly, but were intimately involved in the political events of their times. Isaiah ben Amoz is a paradigmatic case: he is described as meeting with the kings of Judah to advise them on international politics, and he articulates a vision of YHWH that emphasizes the deity's royal attributes. Jeremiah is described as engaged with political events in the early sixth century, albeit from more of an outsider perspective; the prophet Nathan is concerned with King David (2 Sam 7; 12; 1 Kgs 1); and Elijah and his contest with the prophets of Baal is both religious and political in scope (1 Kgs 18). Confirming the link between prophetic activity and periods of political tumult is the lack of prophetic literature relating to periods of relative political quiet.

It is equally clear that, when politics and prophets were active, there could be significant differences of opinion among persons claiming to speak for the deity. Ahaz refuses to receive a sign from Isaiah (7:12); and Isaiah condemns efforts to seek advice from the dead instead of YHWH (8:19–22). He seems to have viewed his entire ministry as one in which he was not heard or understood (6:9–10). Elijah and the prophets of Baal (1 Kgs 18) are a famous case of competing prophetic worldviews; later, Jeremiah disputed the claims of prophets in Jerusalem (Hananiah) and Babylon (Zedekiah and Ahab) that exile and Babylonian dominance would be short-lived (Jer 27–29).

Such competing claims naturally raised questions about how to discern true prophecy from false. Deuteronomy 18 offered two tests that any true, valid prophecy must pass. First, it must be spoken in the name of YHWH; any prophet who speaks in the name of other gods certainly speaks falsely. Second, a prophet who speaks in the name of YHWH must speak words that can be later confirmed as coming to pass or otherwise true. This principle lies behind Isaiah's instruction to 'Bind up the testimony, seal the teaching among my disciples' (8:16, cf. 8:1-2) – he expected to be vindicated in the long run, but needed a record of his words to be preserved in order for this to happen. The records were to serve 'as a witness forever' (30:8). It also undergirds the example that Jeremiah makes of the prophet Hananiah, who prophesies that the temple vessels and the people who were deported in 597 will be brought back within two years; if events do not come to pass as the prophet predicts – as in this case they do not – then the prophet who uttered these words is a false prophet (Jer 28:2–4).[1] Yet, even Deuteronomy's apparently straightforward tests could prove problematic. How long should people wait to see whether a prophet's words come true?

Given these differences of opinion and the difficulty of determining whose word was correct, prophets were obliged to compete to get a hearing, and many of them engaged in quite bizarre behaviours to attract people's attention. A prophet from Mari (a city on the Euphrates, on the border between modern Syria and Iraq) consumed a live (or perhaps raw) lamb in the city gate. Isaiah ben Amoz is said to have gone around Jerusalem naked for three years (Isa 20). Ezekiel lies on his side for more than a year, makes or draws a model city with an iron wall signifying a siege, bakes bread over excrement, shaves then burns and scatters his own hair, and digs through a wall and drags his baggage around to signify defeat and deportation (Ezek 4–5; 12). Jeremiah buries his clothes near the Euphrates, is forbidden to marry, visits a potter and breaks a jug, and carries a yoke to signify submission to Babylonia (Jer 13; 16; 18–19; 28). Hosea marries a woman of ill-repute and has children with symbolically loaded names (Hos 1; 3). These strange activities – known as 'sign-acts' – suggest that prophetic communication, though largely verbal, relied also on the physical presence of the prophet. Though the prophetic literature encourages an interpretive focus on prophetic words, those words were often accompanied by embodied messages.

Although little is known of most ancient prophets' personal lives – and the information provided by the prophetic books should be sifted critically – they seem to have been a reasonably diverse bunch. Some are described as having a special relationship with the deity or as exhibiting especially intense forms of religious behaviour, including dreams, visions or voices – but equally not all of the prophets seem to have felt particularly close to YHWH. Jeremiah, in particular, appears to have had an especially tumultuous relationship with the God for whom he spoke. Some appear to have attracted

---

[1] All dates are BCE unless otherwise specified.

followers to their charismatic personalities; others appear to have been quite solitary. As noted, there is a hint that a prophet's disciples might have been involved in the preservation of his oracles (Isa 8:16); it has been frequently suggested that successive generations of these disciples may stand behind the preservation and development of the Isaianic tradition.

Prophets have sometimes been cast as having a special kind of theological genius, especially in regard to the 'invention' of monotheism. More typically, however, they relied heavily on existing theological language and ideas, rather than inventing new ones. Isaiah ben Amoz made use of existing ideas about the significance of the city of Jerusalem ('Zion'), for example, and relies heavily on shared expectations about the enactment of social justice – the issue was not that his audience was unaware of Yhwh's commitment to justice, but rather that the people knew and were failing to respond appropriately.

Prophets' relationships with major social institutions, especially the temple and the palace, appear also to have been variable. There are some signs of prophetic activity in cultic settings, as when psalms shift from laments and pleas for justice to joyous acclamations of praise (e.g. Pss 6; 28); a prophetic oracle conveyed to the worshipper might explain these shifts in tone. Some psalms explicitly include a brief word from Yhwh that may have been conveyed by a prophet (Pss 12; 60; 91), and others refer to or imply cultic officials with prophetic functions (Pss 81:6–11; 91:15). The prophetic books also contain significant amounts of liturgical material, including hymns, prayers and laments (Isa 38; 49, etc.; Jer 11–20; Hab 3; Jon 2).

At times – especially in periods of anti-Catholic sentiment among Protestant biblical interpreters – it has been popular to pit prophets against priests, envisioning them as antagonists in the battle for Israel's religious soul. The limited evidence for such a sharp distinction is countered by the extensive evidence for close connections between priests and prophets: Jeremiah and Ezekiel come from priestly families, Samuel is trained by Eli the priest, Haggai and Zechariah are probably connected to the cult, and Isaiah ben Amoz has a vision of Yhwh in the temple. When Amos declares that God despises the people's festivals and refuses their offerings, he is not condemning religion as such, but rather the people's inattention to justice in the midst of their revelry (5:21–24). Although the prophets often criticize cultic practice, this should usually be understood as critique that presupposes the extant cultic structure, not as implying incompatibility between prophetic and priestly religion.

As already noted, prophets appear also to have been active in royal settings; they appear frequently in the company of Israel's and Judah's leaders, consulting on the conduct of war, the processes for identifying rightful kings, and providing judgement on royal individuals. Isaiah ben Amoz is intimate with Ahaz and Hezekiah; Nathan with David; and Samuel is central to the stories of the origins of Israelite monarchy. Though prophets are at times the voice 'crying out in the wilderness' (Isa 40:3, as [mis]interpreted by Matt 3:3; Mark 1:3; Luke 3:4; John 1:23) – outsiders critiquing society's powerful insiders – they are just as often at the centre of power, offering criticism from the inside.

Finally, the English term 'prophecy' emphasizes the future in a way that the ancient terms for prophetic figures do not. Although prophetic figures certainly claimed to predict the outcome of certain courses of action, these predictions were usually chronologically close at hand – apart from the difficulty of verifying prophetic declarations concerning the distant future, prophetic speech was simply most relevant when it spoke to people's current times and contexts. Prophetic remarks about the future also normally arise in the context of comments on the present: the reason that prophets discuss the future is usually to warn of the consequences of the people's present activities, with a mind towards changing the future by changing present actions. The role of a prophet was not to foretell future events for their own sake, but to try to warn people of the future that will come about if they continue to act in the way that they are. In this regard, prophets may be understood as astute, theologically informed social and political commentators, who observe their times with a heightened perception of the relationship among acts and consequences and seek to call their contemporaries towards a way of life that places the divine will at the fore.

Prophetic literature

Most prophets probably originally conveyed their messages orally, but all of the surviving evidence concerning these prophets and their messages now exists only in writing, having been preserved in lengthy collections of oracles and narratives.

The early stages in the formation of these long prophetic books should be understood in light of what we know about the compilation and editing of other ancient prophetic collections (de Jong). In the case of the prophecies of Isaiah ben Amoz, contemporary evidence for the collection of prophecies in the Assyrian royal court is especially illuminating. There, prophetic oracles were initially preserved in daily records, some of which were later compiled for longer-term preservation and for performance on special occasions. (Recall that the preserved oracles are heavily concerned with the legitimacy and security of the Assyrian king's rule; recitation of favourable oracles at important state events and celebrations would have helped to reinforce the king's status and his perception as ruling by the gods' will.)

It may be that in some cases the prophet him- or herself was able to write some of this oracular material down. In other cases, the message may have been written down by a scribe. Unlike today, the majority of people in the ancient world were unable to read or write. When Isaiah refers to a physical copy of his testimony it is often with imperatives, telling others what to do with it; although hardly conclusive, this suggests that the production and care of these materials may have been mainly entrusted to others. Jeremiah also instructs someone else to write down and look after his words (Jer 36:2–4, 27–32), although there are a couple of indications that he might have been able to write himself (51:60; cf. 30:2). It is perhaps significant that the prophetic book most widely viewed as being primarily a written work is Ezekiel, whose namesake is said to have been among the priests of the Jerusalem temple: in the ancient world, temples were one of the major sites of scribal education.

Whether Isaiah ben Amoz's prophecies were initially recorded by court scribes or by Isaiah and his disciples (8:1, 16; 30:8), the book's existence indicates that at some point they were viewed as having been validated by subsequent events: the warnings Isaiah ben Amoz had issued about the consequences of Judah's kings' persistent failure to trust in Yhwh and the people's perversion of justice were received, in light of the kingdom's later troubles, as having been true warnings from Yhwh. For this reason, Isaiah's surviving oracles were collected together and preserved. Indisputably, a collection of Isaiah's oracles from the eighth century underwent extensive editing and expansion, on the way to becoming the extant book of Isaiah. However, the extent and nature of this editing is a matter of significant contention.

In addition to oracular material, many prophetic books include stories about the prophet. These narratives make no claim to be the prophet's own words, but suggest that information about the prophet and what he did was sometimes thought to be important. Many narratives recount symbolic prophetic activity, or draw connections between the life of the prophet and his message. There is a substantial amount of such material in the book of

Jeremiah, a limited amount of it in Isaiah, and none at all in books such as Nahum and Malachi. The third-person narration of such material attests to the involvement of others, apart from the prophet, in the production of prophetic books.

Even with larger prophetic collection such as Isaiah or Ezekiel, it is clear that not everything the prophet ever said has been included in the book that bears his name. The process of preserving any prophetic words in writing, however, suggests that someone thought that these words might be of interest to someone who was not present to hear the prophet utter them himself.

The time and expense of literary production in the ancient world was substantial, and preserving prophetic literature required new investment each time a scroll wore out and had to be replaced. Each generation had its own reasons for preserving a prophetic text. Sometimes those reasons, or clues about those reasons, are visible in the form of the interpretive material contained within them. The book of Isaiah is an especially good example: later parts of the book are constantly interpreting and reinterpreting elements of the First Isaiah traditions, explaining how the words of a long-dead prophet still have something to say to subsequent generations. An oft-cited example involves the disability language in Isaiah ben Amoz's call vision, which is used to speak metaphorically about the people's inability to hear the divine word. In the vision, Isaiah is told to

> Go and say to this people:
> 'Keep listening, but do not comprehend;
>   keep looking, but do not understand.'
> Make the mind of this people dull,
>   and stop their ears,
>   and shut their eyes,
> so that they may not look with their eyes,
>   and listen with their ears,
> and comprehend with their minds,
>   and turn and be healed. (6:9–10)

Later parts of the book pick up on this language, implicitly acknowledging that it was the people's inability to see or hear the divine will that led to their judgement – even as they express a hope that the current generation will be able to do otherwise. Second Isaiah describes the role of YHWH's servant as 'a light to the nations, to open the eyes that are blind, to bring out the prisoners from the dungeon, from the prison those who sit in darkness' (42:6–7), as it looks forward to the time that 'the glory of YHWH shall be revealed, and all people shall see it together' (40:5). Similarly, as it imagines the complete rejuvenation of creation, Isa 35:5 declares that 'then the eyes of the blind shall be opened, and the ears of the deaf unstopped'.

These and numerous other passages in the book interpret, reinterpret and build on the words of Isaiah ben Amoz, examining how the people who once were blind and deaf might come to see and to hear the word of God. Later parts of the book also pick up and develop Isaiah ben Amoz's language about the significance of YHWH's holiness, YHWH's role as creator of and ruler over the whole world, and YHWH's election of Israel as his particular people. In each case, these later author-editors sought to emphasize and explain the significance of Isaiah ben Amoz's work to successive generations. As the examples regarding blindness and vision indicate, this work could use and build on the older work even as it transformed it.

Similar interpretive activities are visible throughout all the prophetic books. A passage in Jeremiah describes the phenomenon explicitly:

> Jeremiah took another scroll and gave it to the secretary Baruch son of Neriah, who wrote on it at Jeremiah's dictation all the words of the scroll that King Jehoiakim of Judah had burned in the fire; and many similar words were added to them. (36:32)

Though it may or may not be an accurate description of the origins of the Jeremiah traditions, the episode clearly envisions that the scrolls containing prophets' words would and could be copied anew, as older copies were damaged or wore out, and that this process could involve the addition of further material. The scribes responsible for the preservation of the prophetic material thus played an important role in its interpretation and augmentation.

This process complicates scholars' ability to understand what historical prophets in ancient Israel and Judah were actually like, because the prophets and their activities can only now be viewed through many layers of interpretation. Indeed, it is impossible to know whether any of the words preserved by the tradition are the exact words that Isaiah ben Amoz said on the streets of Jerusalem. The first scribe may already have elected to revise Isaiah's own words at points, for clarity; certainly, later scribes made annotations explaining words that had gone out of use and statements that were no longer clear.

One of the most famous examples of this kind of addition occurs at the end of Isa 6, where the final phrase, 'the holy seed is its stump', identifies the post-exilic community in Judah as the last surviving remnant of the people to whom Isaiah ben Amoz had prophesied judgement. In the process, it injects a small grain of hope into an otherwise doom-laden passage. As such cases make clear, the words written down by Isaiah, his scribe, or his disciples in the eighth century were received and reinterpreted by later generations. Unlike modern commentaries, where such interpretations are placed in a separate book, these early stages of interpretation and reinterpretation are preserved within the primary text. The further annotations were meant to help later readers understand what Isaiah ben Amoz said and how those words might relate to their own context.

There has been much speculation over who preserved Isaiah's words, because the book gives no clear answers. Whoever they were, their interventions have played a role in how those words would be received. The book's contours are very broadly chronological, but they are by no means consistently so. Within each section and in the book overall, the scribe(s) made decisions about which utterances to place alongside each other, influencing how the book's readers would connect one oracle to another, and thus how they might understand one oracle as illuminating another. These were no mindless copyists, but creative writers in their own right.

Teasing apart these layers of interpretation is a monumental task. It is nevertheless an important one, because it matters for understanding that texts be read in their original contexts, as well as in the contexts of the later compilations. The following chapters are an attempt to do just that: although a book of this size cannot go into the processes of Isaiah's formation in detail, the roots of the chapters that follow are sunk deeply in historical context, as they lay out the ways in which each successive generation understood and expanded the message of Isaiah ben Amoz.

Further reading

Blenkinsopp, Joseph. *A History of Prophecy in Israel*. Rev. ed. Louisville, KY: Westminster John Knox, 1996.

Nissinen, Martti. *Prophets and Prophecy in the Ancient Near East*. Atlanta, GA: Society of Biblical Literature, 2019.

Petersen, David L. *The Prophetic Literature: An Introduction*. Louisville, KY: Westminster John Knox, 2002.

Stökl, Jonathan, and Corrine L. Carvalho, eds. *Prophets Male and Female: Gender and Prophecy in the Hebrew Bible, the Eastern Mediterranean, and the Ancient Near East*. Atlanta, GA: Society of Biblical Literature, 2013.

Stulman, Louis, and Hyun Chul Paul Kim. *You Are My People: An Introduction to Prophetic Literature*. Nashville, TN: Abingdon, 2010.

1

Isaiah in the eighth century

'First Isaiah' (Isa 1–39) contains material from a number of different historical periods. Some of this material will be dealt with later in this volume, as part of its attempt to sketch the book of Isaiah's chronological development and its responses to changing historical circumstances.

The core of these chapters may be associated with the prophet Isaiah ben ('son of') Amoz, or 'Isaiah of Jerusalem', who lived and worked in the eighth century. Isaiah ben Amoz is named in several headings as the prophetic mediator of the material that follows (1:1; 2:1; 13:1; 20:2; 37:2), and his activities are reported in a number of narrative passages (Isa 7–8; 20; 36–39). He is therefore usually presumed to be the 'I' in passages that speak in a first-person human voice (Isa 6; 8; 21:8) and the prophet to whom the great complex of theological literature that is the book of Isaiah may ultimately be traced. Although some scholars would limit the surviving work of Isaiah ben Amoz to just a handful of verses, it seems likely that large portions of Isa 3–23 and Isa 28–31 are attributable to him, or perhaps to his immediate disciples (8:1, 16). The corpus of such passages is sometimes called 'Proto-Isaiah'.

A number of much later, legendary traditions attempt to fill in the limited biographical information given by the biblical text. The Babylonian Talmud identifies Isaiah's father Amoz with the brother of Amaziah, king of Judah (b. Meg. 10b), while the tradition that he was martyred by Manasseh by being sawn in half is attested in a number of Hellenistic-period and later texts with varying details (including the *Martyrdom of Isaiah*, *Lives of the Prophets*, the Talmuds, patristic literature and probably Heb 11:37). The latter portion of the *Martyrdom*, known as the *Vision of Isaiah*, takes the prophet on a visionary journey in which he ascends through the seven heavens, a common structure for apocalypses of the period.

In the biblical texts, Isaiah ben Amoz is firmly rooted in the events of his own historical context. The passages associated with him speak to the political tumult of Judah's first significant encounters with the Neo-Assyrian (hereafter Assyrian) Empire, in the mid- to late eighth century, and address political concerns as well as the religious and cultural consequences of these encounters. The theological through-lines of this material concern the sovereignty of YHWH and the expression of the Israelites' loyalty to YHWH through right conduct.

Historical context

Isaiah ben Amoz seems to have had a lengthy career. Isaiah 6:1 refers to a vision that took place in 'the year King Uzziah died', that is, 742. Other early sections of the book contain prophecies about political events over a number of years, from the Syro-Ephraimite Crisis of 734–731 (e.g. Isa 7), to the Ashdod Affair of 714–712 (Isa 20), to the siege of Sennacherib in 701 (e.g. Isa 10; 22:8-11; 29:1-8; 36–37). As this summary suggests, Isaiah ben Amoz's work was intimately caught up with the historical and political events of his day; knowledge of the sequence and major causes of these events is crucial to understanding this work.

Each of these episodes involved the Assyrian Empire, the single most significant political force of the ancient world from the mid-ninth through to the mid-seventh century. There are numerous references to Assyria in the Proto-Isaianic materials, describing the empire as 'the rod of [YHWH's] anger' (10:5) and as the 'bee' that YHWH summons to do his bidding (7:18). As these descriptions suggest, the material associated with Isaiah ben Amoz interprets Assyria's growing power as controlled by and used for the purposes of YHWH. Usually, these purposes involve divine judgement upon the kingdoms of Israel and Judah, manifest as political and military defeat by the Assyrian army.

The rise of the Assyrian Empire and the challenges its interference posed for Judahite political theology appear to have been a major impetus for Isaiah ben Amoz's prophetic activities (Aster). As noted in the Introduction, prophetic activity is associated with periods of political uncertainty and upheaval. International interference in Judah's domestic affairs seems to have provoked socio-economic problems, popular unrest, and prophetic reactions.

Prior to the mid-ninth century, the traditional imperial powers of Egypt and Mesopotamia had been preoccupied closer to their homelands for several centuries, with little interest in exerting their influence over the southern Levant (the region on the eastern edge of the Mediterranean). Assyria's Shalmaneser III (r. 858–824) clashed with a coalition of western kings, including Ahab of Israel (r. 869–850), in 853, though there is no record of tribute payments until the reign of Jehu (r. 843–815), and the empire's westward efforts stalled for much of the next century. This long period of international neglect enabled a number of small kingdoms to flourish, including Judah and the northern kingdom of Israel.

The Assyrians resumed their expansionary efforts in the middle of the eighth century, under Tiglath-pileser III (r. 745–727). He re-subdued Babylonia to the south and Urartu in the mountainous region to Assyria's north, then campaigned into the Levant, taking tribute from Menahem of Israel (r. 745–737). Such payments avoided continued antagonism and guaranteed Assyrian support for the king in power – provided he continued to make them. In these early stages, the effects of Assyrian ambition were felt most acutely by the northern territories of Aram and Israel. Judah's more southern location, together with Israel's position as a buffer state, meant that Judah was at first largely shielded from direct influence of Assyrian power.

This changed in the 730s. The kings who had earlier submitted to Assyrian authority were increasingly obliged to levy heavy taxes on major landowners in order to muster the funds needed to ensure Assyrian support for their rule (as reflected later in 2 Kgs 15:19–20). There is also evidence that the state was trying to manipulate agricultural production for its own financial benefit, discouraging the subsistence cultivation that ensured the people had food to eat in favour of the specialized production of revenue-producing crops capable of funding the Assyrian tribute payments. Simultaneously, the royal court and the elite merchant class benefited from control over increased trade in the region. The economic inequalities that resulted are a major focus of the eighth-century prophetic literature (Mic 2:1–2; Isa 5:8, etc.)

In an attempt to rid themselves of this onerous tribute system, Pekah of Israel (r. 736–732) and a coalition of other Levantine kings joined together to try to push off Assyrian control. Hoping to present a united Levantine front, Pekah and the other principal leader of the coalition, Rezin of Damascus (r. 754–732), invited Judah to join the cause. Ahaz of Judah (r. 735–715), however, refused. This triggered threats and military manoeuvres designed to force Judah's compliance. Pekah and Rezin attacked Jerusalem in 734, intending to replace Ahaz with a ruler more sympathetic to the coalition's goals (2 Kgs 16:5–9; Isa 7). This is the context of the sign promised to Ahaz in Isa 7: Yhwh tells the king that he has nothing to fear because these two kings and their kingdoms will soon be in ruins, defeated by the Assyrians (7:16; 8:4). The episode is known as the 'Syro-Ephraimitic Crisis' (sometimes referred to as the 'Syro-Ephraimite War', although there was not active warfare for the whole of the period), after the main players of the coalition: Pekah's northern kingdom of Israel was often referred to poetically as 'Ephraim', and the Aramean king Rezin ruled the area now known as Syria.

Tiglath-pileser defeated the coalition in his western campaign of 734–731. He killed Rezin and Pekah, conquered their cities, and took enormous sums of gold, silver, and other goods as tribute before incorporating vast swathes of coalition territory as provinces under direct Assyrian control. He installed an Assyrian governor in Damascus and a puppet king, Hoshea (r. 732–724), in Samaria, to oversee what remained of the quasi-independent kingdom of Israel.

The threat that the coalition posed to Assyrian power in the region meant that Tiglath-pileser would probably have shown up to deal with it of his own accord. Yet the biblical accounts report that Ahaz was so fearful that he sent envoys to Assyria pre-emptively, promising to submit to Assyrian authority if Tiglath-pileser and his army would rid him of the coalition besieging Jerusalem and ensure that he retained the throne. As a consequence of the Syro-Ephraimite Crisis, therefore, Judah came under direct Assyrian authority for the first time. It would remain an Assyrian vassal kingdom for more than a century, until the empire's demise in the last third of the seventh century.

Assyria's impact on Judah became even more direct a decade and a half later, when the rump state that had survived in the environs of Samaria was obliterated completely. Tiglath-pileser had died in 727; as was quite typical of imperial subordinates then and in the centuries to follow, the northern kingdom saw a chance of regaining its independence while the new Assyrian king, Shalmaneser V (r. 726–722), was finding his feet. In what would become a recurring pattern in both Israel and Judah over the subsequent two centuries, Hoshea sought help from Egypt for his rebellion (2 Kgs 17:4).

Empires are short-lived if they do not respond to such efforts, and within a year or two Shalmaneser had established himself well enough to reassert his authority by laying siege to Samaria. The city fell to Assyria in 721. It is not quite clear whether the victorious king was Shalmaneser or his brother, Sargon II (r. 721–705), as the former ruled only briefly before being overthrown by the latter. The details of this overthrow are unclear and very little in the way of textual evidence regarding Shalmaneser's activities has survived; he seems to have died or disappeared right around the time the city fell. The biblical texts report a three-year siege, which would put its start in 724. The annals from Sargon's reign suggest that he inherited Shalmaneser's war and seized it as an opportunity to demonstrate his own authority.

The fact that Samaria had already tried to push off Assyrian authority before, in the 730s, meant the Assyrians viewed the situation in the 720s as requiring a massive show of power, aimed at the surrounding kingdoms as a warning of the consequences for rebellion. What remained of the northern kingdom was brought under direct Assyrian control, and an Assyrian eunuch was placed in charge of the new province of Samerina. Sargon claimed that he deported more than 27,000 people and brought deportees from other parts of the empire into the territory to replace them. These population exchanges, as well as the religious and cultural changes associated with them, are recalled in 2 Kgs 17:24–41. The account is doubtless coloured by later animosities over distinct southern and northern ways of worshipping YHWH – such differences are traced to the foreign origins of the people living in Samerina, for whom the Assyrians are said to have fetched a deported priest back from exile, to teach the foreigners how to worship YHWH – but they attest to the Assyrians' remarkable power to remake the demography of the empire.

Sargon's seizure of Samaria marked the end of the northern kingdom of Israel as an independent state. Apart from brief periods under the Hasmoneans (140–63 BCE) and Bar Kokba (132–153 CE), the region would remain under the authority of foreign empires until the twentieth century. There are fewer passages in Isaiah that seem to deal with these events than with ones impacting directly on Judah and Jerusalem, but Isaiah ben Amoz's response to them is in keeping with his other words: Samaria's defeat was due to its failure to trust in YHWH. Its leaders relied on their own military strength and on political alliances instead of relying on YHWH (9:8 [ET]-10:4).

In the wake of the northern kingdom's dissolution, the new Assyrian province of Samerina was directly on Judah's doorstep, just a few miles north of Jerusalem. The Neo-Assyrian Empire had strong diplomatic interests in facilitating trade, and over the next hundred years it fostered and exploited growth in Judah's contacts with the wider Near Eastern world; ambassadors and envoys, merchants and traders would have come through Jerusalem in large numbers. The anxiety about Yahwistic distinctiveness that characterizes the book of Deuteronomy is a response to such interactions, as exposure to different cultural and religious practices posed a temptation to the people of Jerusalem and the surrounding countryside. There are hints of similar concerns about foreign religious practices in Isaiah, usually in connection with the prophet's opposition to foreign alliances (Isa 20; 28; 30).

Assyria's looming presence in the region crept still closer to Jerusalem in the 710s, as a series of rebellions among the coastal states between 720 and 710 prompted another Assyrian campaign, resulting in the formation of the province of Ashdod in 711 (cf. Isa 20). Three thousand skeletons buried in a mass grave at Ashdod give an idea of the scale of these rebellions' human toll. These rebellions, like the earlier ones, sought Egyptian aid in their efforts to throw off the Assyrian yoke; some of the smaller kingdoms in the area, including Judah, were almost certainly lobbied for support as well. Oracles and sign-acts warning of Egypt's unreliability likely relate to these years (Isa 18–20).

In his royal inscriptions, Sargon claims that he summoned all the western kings to attend the dedication of the city of Dur Sharrukin (modern Khorsabad) in 706. Though he is not explicitly named, it is possible that Hezekiah of Judah (r. 715–687) and members of his royal court were among those present. In the Assyrian heartland, they would have seen first-hand the Assyrians' monumental palace architecture, designed to intimidate and impress visitors: enormous winged bulls guarding doorways, wall reliefs depicting successful military campaigns, and cuneiform texts recounting the king's achievements, legible only to the initiated. The scale and splendour of these Assyrian palaces was unmatched anywhere else in the empire.

Despite these impressive building projects, Sargon was mortal. He met his end on the battlefield in 705, and his body was never recovered – a uniquely awful fate for an Assyrian king, who would have looked forward to a sumptuous afterlife provisioned by supplicants at his royal tomb. It likely prompted a celebration in Judah (Isa 14), and it certainly prompted Hezekiah (r. 715–687) to repeat the by-now-familiar pattern of forming an anti-Assyrian coalition and withholding tribute. Sargon's successor, Sennacherib (r. 705–681) was not free to campaign to the west until 701 – but upon his arrival the consequences were disastrous. His annals record forty-six Judahite cities as having been pillaged and claim that he took more than two hundred thousand people and animals as spoil (though this is generally considered an exaggeration). Lavish reliefs from Sennacherib's palace at Nineveh (now in the British Museum) depict the siege and capture of the city of Lachish, Judah's most important city after Jerusalem. The capital itself was probably also besieged; the annals describe Hezekiah as shut up in Jerusalem 'like a bird in a cage'. Isaiah described Jerusalem as like 'a shelter in a cucumber field' (1:8) – the only thing in Judah left standing.

Surprisingly, Judah survived Sennacherib's assault; although it was stripped of much of its territory – like Samaria three decades earlier – Jerusalem was left intact and the kingdom permitted to continue as an independent vassal state, rather than becoming a province under direct Assyrian rule.

The exact reasons for Hezekiah's survival are disputed, even within the biblical tradition, which preserves at least three different accounts of the rebellion and its aftermath. Although the two preserved in the book of Isaiah were probably written many years later, they are in keeping with the emphasis on trust in Yhwh that characterizes the eighth-century material. In the first, Yhwh provokes rumours of problems elsewhere in the empire, meant to prompt Sennacherib to abandon his efforts in Judah (Isa 37:1–9; 2 Kgs 19:6–9). The narrative, which is certainly composite, implies that this provided only a temporary reprieve while the Assyrian king went off to deal with issues on the Philistine coast and in Egypt.

It is followed by a second account of the city's salvation, in which Hezekiah is shown appealing to Yhwh to defend the city and thereby demonstrate that Yhwh's power is greater than that of the Assyrians' gods or the gods of other nations (Isa 37:14–20; 2 Kgs 19:15–19). Yhwh responds with an oracle against the Assyrian king, delivered via Isaiah ben Amoz (Isa 37:21–29; 2 Kgs 19:20–28). Assyrian success against Jerusalem would have been seen as confirmation of the power of Assyria and its gods; this being an affront to Yhwh's own authority, Yhwh declares that 'I will defend this city to save it, for my own sake and for the sake of my servant David' (Isa 37:35; 2 Kgs 19:34). This is followed by direct divine intervention, with an angel of Yhwh causing the deaths of 185,000 soldiers in the Assyrian camp (Isa 37:36; 2 Kgs 19:35). This account also implies that Sennacherib's (much) later assassination was punishment for attacking Jerusalem (Isa 37:37–38; 2 Kgs 19:36–37). Both of these accounts of the invasion explain Sennacherib's withdrawal from Jerusalem with reference to the city's unique status before Yhwh: because of the temple on Mount Zion and Yhwh's special relationship with the Davidic king, Yhwh would not allow the city to fall.

The Assyrians had sent the Rabshakeh, a high official of the empire who governed a large territory, and whose title literally meant 'chief water-bearer'; he had taunted Hezekiah's representatives with claims that Yhwh was in fact on the Assyrian side, and that their arrival was punishment for Hezekiah's attempts to centralize the worship of Yhwh in Jerusalem (Isa 36:4–10; 2 Kgs 18:19–25). These efforts are presented by the biblical texts as an outworking of Hezekiah's piety (2 Kgs 18:3–7). More pragmatically, it has been suggested that dismantling local worship sites around this time may have been part of an attempt to protect these local altars from being desecrated or destroyed by an Assyrian army on the rampage. The altar at Tel Arad, for example, appears to have been decommissioned at this time, but there is no sign that it was violently destroyed, as might have been expected if this were part of a theologically motivated purge (compare 2 Kgs 23:4–20). Whatever the original reasons for these changes, the texts present Yhwh's defence of Jerusalem and its king as part of the tradition's wider support of exclusive worship in Jerusalem.

In political terms, the most plausible explanation of Hezekiah's escape from Assyrian punishment suggests that, after Sennacherib's army arrived and wreaked havoc on the surrounding countryside, the Judahite king elected to cut his losses, capitulate and pay heavy tribute. This version is not included in the book of Isaiah but appears briefly in 2 Kings 18, where Hezekiah is reported to have appealed to the Assyrian king, claiming, 'I have done wrong; withdraw from me; whatever you impose on me I will bear' (2 Kgs 18:14). Sennacherib demands vast sums of silver and gold, which Hezekiah supplies by stripping the temple and royal treasuries. The Assyrian annals add jewels and Hezekiah's daughters to the list of 'gifts' by which Hezekiah ensured his survival.

Notably, they do not claim that Sennacherib destroyed the city. Indeed, the king may not himself have bothered to come to Jerusalem, delegating negotiations to the Rabshakeh and other officials, instead (Isa 36:2–20; 2 Kgs 18:17–35). Both the annals and the biblical texts suggest that Sennacherib was also dealing with rebellions elsewhere in the empire; under pressure, he may have decided that a hefty monetary penalty and the devastation already wreaked in the countryside was a good enough guarantee of Hezekiah's future compliance, and that tying up troops in a prolonged siege was not worth the risk to other parts of the empire. It has also been suggested that Sennacherib might have been lenient because he had a Judahite wife or concubine. Assyrian kings at times took elite women from client states as plunder, and royal tombs bearing at least one West Semitic woman's name have been discovered at an earlier palace in Nimrud (Calaḫ). Without further evidence, this remains only an intriguing hypothesis.

Both the annals and the biblical texts also suggest that Hezekiah's rebellion was part of his attempts to exert political pressure on the surrounding territories. Second Kings 18:8 refers to Hezekiah attacking the Philistines, while the annals indicate that Hezekiah and his anti-Assyrian allies had captured Padi, the king of Ekron and a loyal Assyrian vassal, and were holding him hostage in Jerusalem, having deposed him in favour of someone more favourable to revolt. This explains at least one of the consequences of Sennacherib's subsequent invasion, namely, that Judah was stripped of its western territory in the Shephelah: the region that bordered on Philistia. Ekron, a major city in this area, had sometimes been under Judahite influence; now, it and its enormous olive oil production centre were placed firmly in Philistine control.

All the sources agree that Jerusalem was spared destruction and that Hezekiah was allowed to remain on the throne. The Assyrian inscriptions present the outcome as a success, insofar as it achieved the subordination of Hezekiah and Judah, without claiming that Sennacherib actually destroyed the city. The biblical traditions take the city's survival as an opportunity to demonstrate a theological point concerning Jerusalem's special status and Yhwh's willingness to intervene on its behalf.

The episode has continued to inspire authors through the ages. The English Romantic poet Lord Byron imagined Assyria's assault and Jerusalem's salvation in his poem *The Destruction of Sennacherib*. Its famous opening lines also seem to allude to Isa 5:29–30's description of the Assyrian military:

> The Assyrian came down like the wolf on the fold,
> And his cohorts were gleaming in purple and gold;
> And the sheen of their spears was like stars on the sea,
> When the blue wave rolls nightly on deep Galilee.

Clearly Jerusalem's deliverance was poignant in its own time as well, though the belief that Yhwh would never allow the city to fall to invaders would prove problematic later in Judah's history, when it created false hopes concerning the Babylonian sieges of Jerusalem in 597 and 586. That the city was ultimately destroyed provoked a theological crisis, and parts of Second Isaiah continue to reflect back on the city's defeat at that time.

Although the biblical texts obscure the fact through their emphasis on Jerusalem's survival, the kingdom as a whole suffered badly as a result of the campaign. After 701, Hezekiah's kingdom was little more than a rump state centred on Jerusalem; although the capital may have grown because of an influx of refugees, all of Judah's other major cities had been dismantled by Sennacherib and all of its lowland territory had been handed over to Philistia. Of more than three hundred settlements extant prior to the invasion, fewer than forty survived. As noted above, it is possible that the accounts of Hezekiah's cult centralization (2 Kgs 18:3–4) are an attempt to make a virtue out of necessity; with all other religious sites of any significance destroyed, Jerusalem became the de facto centre of the Yahwistic cult.

Theological themes and concerns

These political and social circumstances in the second half of the eighth century dominate the theological profile of Isaiah ben Amoz. The prophet's activity is intensely concerned with the activities of Judah's kings, paying particular attention to whether they place their trust in Yhwh or rely on human allies when faced with external political threats, and whether they enact the commitments to justice and righteousness that characterize Yhwh himself.

At the heart of the eighth-century Isaiah traditions is the vision account narrated in Isa 6. Although the chapter does not date in its entirety to the eighth century, it provides a good entry into key elements of Isaiah ben Amoz's theology. The chapter is one of three chapters, Isa 6–8, that together are often referred to as the Isaiah Memoir (*Denkschrift*, in German). These chapters have been traditionally linked very closely with Isaiah ben Amoz because Isa 6 and Isa 8 are narrated in the first person: 'I saw Yhwh sitting on a throne' (6:1) ... 'Then Yhwh said to me' (8:1). Passages in the prophetic books that use a first-person voice are widely (though not universally) considered the material most likely to be attributable to the original prophet. (Pseudepigraphical literature – works written in the name of someone else – is more characteristic of the Second Temple period.)

Isaiah 6 is a call narrative, describing the prophet's commissioning as a mediator between the divine and human realm. Other examples of call narratives include Exod 3; 1 Kgs 22; Jer 1; and Ezek 2. A key function of such narratives is to establish the prophet's authority, which exists as an extension and as a representative of divine authority. Like a political ambassador required to present his credentials so that his audience will believe that he is authorized to convey messages the king's behalf, ancient prophets sought to establish their prophetic credentials, in order to be taken seriously as Yhwh's representatives. Describing an audience before Yhwh seems to have been one way of doing this (compare Exod 24:9–11; 1 Kgs 22:19–23; Amos 7:1–9; 8:1–9:4; Ezek 1–3). In keeping with this image, Yhwh is portrayed in Isa 6 as the divine king, complete with supernatural attendants, the seraphim.

Indeed, throughout Isaiah, there is a deeply embedded emphasis on Yhwh as the supreme authority. Any challenge to this authority has serious consequences. Isaiah ben Amoz's message of judgement arises in response to Judah's kings' persistence in political alliances, in which they rely on themselves and other fallible human beings for support rather than on Yhwh.

Isaiah 6 follows a pattern that is fairly typical of most call accounts. First, Yʜᴡʜ confronts Isaiah ben Amoz, informing him of his commission. Isaiah ben Amoz, however, is not enthusiastic: 'Woe is me!' (6:5). More specifically, he protests that he is inadequate to the task: 'I am a man of unclean lips, and I live among a people of unclean lips' (6:5). Yʜᴡʜ deals with that problem by sending one of the seraphs to purify Isaiah ben Amoz's lips (6:6–7); Isaiah ben Amoz concludes that he is up for the job, after all, and volunteers himself when Yʜᴡʜ asks who ought to be sent to speak with the people (6:8).

The message Isaiah ben Amoz is then told to convey might have prompted second thoughts about volunteering. Like most prophets whose traditions have been preserved, he is given a grim job: telling the people that they have so stubbornly refused to pay attention to Yʜᴡʜ's demands that judgement is now inevitable. Modern activists and artists have likened their own sense of calling to Isaiah's in this regard, from Bob Dylan – 'Isaiah the prophet, even Jeremiah, see if their brethren didn't want to bust their brains for telling it right like it is, yeah – these are my roots I suppose' – to U2, whose refrain in 'Sunday Bloody Sunday' recalls Isa 6:11: 'How long? How long must I sing this song?'

Much of the later artistic reception of Isaiah – from Reformation-era woodcuts to the work of Marc Chagall – focuses on this scene, which affords an opportunity to portray the divine throne room, the attending seraphim, and the submission (and subsequent mission) of the prophet. G. F. Handel, who used Isaianic texts extensively in his *Messiah*, is reported to have claimed that he had a vision of 'the great God himself upon his throne', just as Isaiah himself had. Other artistic motifs inspired by Isaiah include the beating of swords into ploughshares (2:4) and the 'peaceable kingdom' (11:6–9); Isaianic texts have also been imported by Christian artists into images of Gabriel's annunciation to Mary (Luke 1, based on Isa 7:14) and Jesus's crucifixion (based on Isa 52:13–53:12).

It is significant that Isaiah ben Amoz's vision of Yʜᴡʜ takes place in the temple: 'I saw Yʜᴡʜ sitting on a throne, high and lofty, and the hem of his robe filled the temple' (6:1). This indicates that the prophet was familiar with the temple precincts, perhaps even its inner sanctum where the cherubim that formed the divine throne were curtained off. At the very least, the role of the temple in Isaiah ben Amoz's call is a salutary reminder that it is more effective to think in terms of complementary human conduits for communication with the divine than it is to think in terms of a priest-versus-prophet antithesis.

The location of the vision in the temple highlights Yhwh's supreme holiness and the significance of this holiness for Isaianic theology. Yhwh's most characteristic epithet in the book of Isaiah, appearing in all of its parts, is 'the Holy One of Israel'. The title is not exclusive to Isaiah – it appears a few times in Psalms and Jeremiah – but its prevalence in this book (24 of its 29 biblical appearances) suggests that it may well have originated with Isaiah ben Amoz himself. The seraphs' acclamation of Yhwh's holiness in the temple vision – 'holy, holy, holy is Yhwh of Hosts' (6:3) – has often been identified as the source of the title, if indeed it did originate with Isaiah ben Amoz. The seraphs' threefold repetition of 'holy' is emphatic: Yhwh is the most holy of the most holy of the most holy. Later, the repetition was read by Christians as a reference to the triune holiness of the Father, Son and Holy Spirit, inspiring Rev 4:8 as well as chants and hymns in the liturgies of the Catholic and Orthodox churches. The seraphs' acclamation was also incorporated into Second Temple Jewish liturgies, at Qumran and elsewhere, and continues to appear in traditional Jewish morning prayers. More recently it has found its way into such classic hymns as 'Holy, Holy, Holy, Lord God Almighty' by Reginald Heber (1783–1826). Indeed, the use of the divine title 'Holy One of Israel' also in the Psalms (Ps 71:22; 78:41; 89:18) might indicate that it was a title originally used in the Jerusalem temple, which Isaiah ben Amoz adopted and popularized. Whatever its origins, Isaiah's frequent description of Yhwh as 'the Holy One of Israel' is a sign of the importance of the concept in Isaiah ben Amoz's theology.

The holiness and incomparable otherness of Yhwh is also a major theme of priestly theologies, and is especially characteristic of priestly legal traditions in the Pentateuch. Although much of that material was written down later than the time of Isaiah ben Amoz, it provides a glimpse of some of the holiness concerns of the Jerusalem priesthood. In the book of Isaiah, as in the priestly literature, Yhwh's holiness is connected to Yhwh's moral vision. As Leviticus puts it, 'I am Yhwh your God; sanctify yourselves therefore, and be holy, for I am holy' (Lev 11:44; cf. 11:45; 19:2; 20:7, 26). Such statements reflect the principle of 'imitation of God' (*imitatio Dei*, in Latin): the idea that one way of discerning right human behaviour is to look to the deity and seek to imitate what one finds there. Because holiness is a prominent aspect of Yhwh's character, Yhwh's people should seek to be holy, too.

Holiness is a potent force. Yhwh's superlative holiness means that impurity – the antithesis of holiness – is an affront to God. By extension, impurity or lack of holiness is problematic for a relationship with the deity.

Insofar as humans are inevitably not perfectly holy, for a human to be in the divine presence is thus quite dangerous there is an inevitable gulf between divine and human holiness. Priestly practices of cleansing and purifying were designed to ensure a basic level of holiness, in order to prevent a disastrous encounter between human and divine. Holiness was also facilitated through the pursuit of justice and righteousness in one's relationships. To fail to maintain holiness in these ways was to risk divine wrath and abandonment.

Unfortunately, the accounts that the Judahites render of themselves in the biblical literature report that the people neglected both the religious rituals and the ethical behaviour that would have kept them holy enough for proximity to YHWH. The rift between YHWH's supreme holiness and the people's lack of holiness is a persistent source of existential danger (5:16–24). Later in Judah's history, this would provide a key explanation for why Jerusalem was destroyed and many of its people deported (Jer 17; Ezek 20; 22). The people's impurity was incompatible with YHWH's presence; without YHWH's presence and protection, the city was doomed.

In Isa 6, the prophet's presence before the superlatively holy YHWH requires that he, too, achieve a minimum level of holiness. In other words, in order for Isaiah ben Amoz to be in YHWH's presence and receive his commission, he has to be purged of his sins. This is the service the seraph provides (6:6). The warning that Isaiah ben Amoz is then told to convey to the people of Judah is that, if they do not likewise meet the minimum standards of holiness necessary for a relationship with YHWH, divine judgement to purge them of their sins will be necessary.

YHWH's presence amongst the people is thus a double-edged sword: a source of divine protection, but also dangerous. This ambiguity is apparent in the famous oracle about the child born to the young woman in Isa 7. The child, Isaiah ben Amoz says, will be called 'Immanu-'El, 'God is with us' (7:14). On the one hand, this is positive, because it represents YHWH's commitment to be present with and protect his people. Yet, at the same time, it acts as a reminder that YHWH's presence has major behavioural implications. If the people fail to adhere to the sort of behaviour required by the holiest of divine presences, there will be terrible consequences. (The hymn 'O Come, O Come Emmanuel' [*Veni, Veni Emmanuel*] derives from this chapter and the next.)

The implications of YHWH's holiness for human behaviour are apparent most clearly in Isaiah ben Amoz's pervasive interest in righteousness (*tsedeqah*) and justice (*mishpat*). These key terms appear repeatedly, beginning with the Song of the Vineyard in Isa 5, in which YHWH compares the behaviour of the people to the stubborn refusal of a cultivated vineyard to produce good grapes: despite YHWH's attention and care, the people pursue violence and bloodshed instead of justice and righteous behaviour (5:7). A major oracle concerning the political, religious, and moral failings likewise identifies justice and righteousness as the plumb-line of YHWH's plans for Zion's judgement: 'I will make justice the line, and righteousness the plummet' (28:17). The lies and the deceit that have rotted the city from the inside out must be purged, if it is to have any future.

Isaiah ben Amoz's concerns about justice appear to have been prompted in part by the socio-economic situation of the late eighth century (Coomber). The middle of the century had been generally peaceful and prosperous, with the political and military quiet of the preceding centuries facilitated a flourishing economy. But a small, wealthy upper class were the primary beneficiaries of these economic opportunities, and this growing economic and social inequality produced an environment ripe for corruption and abuse.

In the Song of the Vineyard, Isaiah ben Amoz pays particular attention to the abuse of power that this social stratification had enabled. He catalogues the greediness of the kingdom's elites, depicting them as grabbing up property and resources to the detriment of those whose livelihoods depend on them – even relying on pernicious practices and outright bribery to get what they want (5:8, 23). These oppressive acts – seizing the fields and houses of the economically marginal, and thus depriving them of their homes and livelihoods – are vividly described and identified as a major cause of Israel's looming demise. The carelessness of the elites for the needs of others is demonstrated by their single-minded pursuit of their own pleasures (5:11–13). Such behaviour is antithetical to YHWH's character and is resoundingly rejected (5:16).

Isaiah ben Amoz was not alone in his concern that YHWH's people were inadequately executing their obligation to pursue lives characterized by justice and righteousness. The prophetic books of Amos and Micah, also associated with the eighth century, show sustained interest in the moral conduct of the people as well. Amos accuses the elites of bribery, judicial corruption, gluttony and defrauding the poor (2:6–8; 4:1; 5:10–12; 6:4–6). Micah is furious at the social and economic elites in Samaria and Jerusalem, who are condemned for their oppression of the weak; like Amos and Isaiah ben Amoz, Micah focuses especially on corruption of judicial procedures and other forms of power abuse (2:1–2, 8–9; 3:2–3, 5, 9–11). Because these prophets understand right conduct as an obligation arising from devotion to YHWH, they repeatedly warn that immoral conduct will lead to divine punishment. That is, right conduct is a religious obligation: a failure on this front thus amounts to rebellion against YHWH, and no pious ritual can redeem those who commit such offences (compare Third Isaiah, Isa 1:10–17; 58:1–9; 65:1–16).

Ignoring the poor, the marginalized, or those who lack family support; turning a blind eye to injustice because it is to one's own advantage – these are anathema to the prophets, including Isaiah ben Amoz. If there is one thing on which the prophets are absolutely consistent, it is that YHWH hates all forms of social injustice, and that those who practice it are condemned. Such words retain much of their discomfiting power even today; there is almost no one who lives comfortably of whom it could not be said, as Isaiah ben Amoz does, 'the spoil of the poor is in your houses' (3:14). One does not have to go out and steal from the poor directly to be guilty of exploitation; the system itself is unjust.

Isaiah ben Amoz's interest in justice and righteousness concerned the behaviour of the people as a whole, but also the behaviour of Israel and Judah's kings, whose commitments to justice and righteousness (or lack thereof) had wide-ranging consequences for the entire community. In the ancient Near East the ideal of kingship was tightly bound to an expectation of royal justice and righteousness, with the king's actions viewed as essential to the kingdom's flourishing. It is as divine king that YHWH is concerned with justice and righteousness. The Judahite kingdom ruled by YHWH's representative is an extension of YHWH's own kingdom; the establishment of justice and righteousness in the human realm therefore reflects on YHWH.

In keeping with this, Isaiah ben Amoz signals that the failure of the northern kingdom of Israel to maintain behaviour appropriate to their relationship with YHWH was a major cause of its demise (9:8–21; 28). The northerners' failure in this regard is presented to the inhabitants of the southern kingdom as an object lesson and warning; if they follow in the northern kingdom's footsteps, they will alienate YHWH and suffer similar consequences.

As this begins to suggest, one of Isaiah ben Amoz's other main concerns is the state of Judah's international politics. Notably, the book depicts the prophet as being intimately involved in the kingdom's political affairs. Unlike Micah, who speaks against the sins of the rich and powerful from the perspective of an outsider, Isaiah ben Amoz is portrayed as a man of influence and power – an advisor to kings, with privileged access to a succession of Judah's monarchs (Isa 7; 36–39). His message to these kings is that they must trust in the power and authority of Yʜwʜ, their divine king, rather than in the limited power of human kings.

When Isaiah ben Amoz's vision account dates itself to 'the year that King Uzziah died' (6:1) – that is, 742 – this is no incidental comment. As noted in the historical overview, this was about the time that the Assyrian Empire began its westward expansion. Although the empire's ambitions are not explicitly present in the vision, its depiction of Yʜwʜ as the divine king, enthroned in Jerusalem, constitutes an implicit challenge to any Assyrian claim to power over the city or its inhabitants. Elsewhere, of course, Isaiah ben Amoz is much more explicit in his assertions of Yʜwʜ's ultimate authority. The Assyrian kings may seem in control of events, but in fact it is Yʜwʜ who is in charge. That the people must therefore trust fully in Yʜwʜ is one of Isaiah ben Amoz's most persistent messages.

This is especially overt in the narrative account of Isaiah ben Amoz's encounter with Ahaz (Isa 7). The chapter refers to Isaiah ben Amoz in the third person, clearly signalling different origins from Isa 6 and 8. Whether it should be taken as a closely contemporary account of Isaiah ben Amoz's interaction with King Ahaz, written by one of Isaiah ben Amoz's disciples, or as a much later addition, is disputed. Isaiah 7 and 36–37 set up a contrast between Ahaz, the king who does not trust in Yʜwʜ, and Hezekiah, the king who does. Since Isa 36–37 is a near (but not exact) duplication of 2 Kgs 18–20, the dating of Isa 7 relies in part on judgements regarding the origins and later revision of the Deuteronomistic History, the account of Israel and Judah's history spanning the books of Joshua-2 Kings.

Though Isa 7 in its current form may indeed come from a later time, it brings into focus the emphasis on trust in Yʜwʜ that characterizes other oracles that may be more confidently assigned to Isaiah ben Amoz, and thus provides a useful window into this aspect of Isaianic theology. The episode is set in the midst of the Syro-Ephraimite Crisis, in which the kings of Israel and Aram – Pekah and Rezin – form an alliance against the Assyrians. Because Judah would not join their alliance, they invaded Judah and sought to depose King Ahaz in favour of a king more amenable to their anti-Assyrian agenda. Ahaz, perhaps unsurprisingly, is fearful of the alliance: he is shaking 'as the trees of the forest shake before the wind' (7:2) – just as one might now describe a frightened person as 'shaking like a leaf'.

Isaiah ben Amoz meets with the king face-to-face, to explain that he need not be fearful if only he will trust Yʜwʜ. The kings who threaten his throne are only human, after all, and their power will soon pass away; Yʜwʜ's power is eternal. In the next chapter Isaiah ben Amoz gives his son a prophetic name, Maher-shalal-hash-baz, 'The Spoil Speeds, the Prey Hastens', in an attempt to convey to Ahaz the inevitability of these two kingdoms' imminent plundering by the Assyrians. The Assyrian triumph will not take long, either: it will take place 'before the child knows how to call "my father" or "my mother"' (8:1–4).

In Isa 7, Isaiah ben Amoz urges Ahaz to stand firm in his faith in Yhwh and thus firm in his confidence concerning Pekah and Rezin's mortal limitations. Isaiah even offers Ahaz a sign from Yhwh that he can trust in him (7:10–11). But Ahaz cannot be dissuaded from his fears and refuses to ask for a sign (7:12). Annoyed at Ahaz's stubbornness, Yhwh sends a sign anyway: the child called 'God is with us' (7:13–16). Thanks to Yhwh's presence among the people, the sign suggests, the city will be saved – the kings now threatening Ahaz will soon be consigned to the dustbin of history.

The Assyrians' involvement was not, of course, entirely a blessing. The account in 2 Kgs 16:7–9 explains the situation in more straightforwardly political terms: rather than taking Isaiah ben Amoz's advice to 'be quiet' and do nothing, Ahaz sent emissaries to the Assyrian king Tiglath-pileser III, begging for help in defending himself against Israel and Aram. In return for the Assyrians' assistance, Ahaz promised loyalty to the Assyrian king – together with significant tribute payments. As a result of Ahaz's fearful actions, Judah became an Assyrian vassal kingdom, a sworn supporter of the empire. In 731, Tiglath-pileser came and wiped out the allied coalition and turned most of its kings' territories into Assyrian provinces. Only the capital of the northern kingdom, Samaria, and a small area around the city survived with a degree of independence – albeit as a vassal state forcibly subjected to Assyrian authority. The oracles against Damascus and Ephraim (17:1–6) likely refer to this period, depicting the two kingdoms' intertwined fates.

One of the striking aspects of Isaiah ben Amoz's advice to Ahaz is that it is both theological and political. Politically, it was in Tiglath-pileser's own interest to eliminate the rebellious alliance of the northern kingdom and the Aramaeans. Judah hardly needed to subject itself to Assyrian imperial authority in order to get the alliance off its back – the Assyrians would almost certainly have turned up to quash the rebellion out of their own imperial self-interest. Ahaz just had to wait it out. Interpreting the political situation theologically, Isaiah ben Amoz presents this as an expression of Yhwh's authority over mortal kings and their machinations: Ahaz need only trust in Yhwh to save him and his kingdom from the Syro-Ephraimite attempts to overrun it.

After the campaign of 731, Tiglath-pileser installed Hoshea as king in Samaria; 2 Kgs 15:30 portrays this as a coup against Pekah. But, within just a few years, Hoshea rebelled against Assyria by seeking support from Egypt (2 Kgs 17:20). In response, the Assyrians returned and besieged Samaria. It took three years – spanning the end of Shalmaneser V's reign and the beginning of Sargon II's – but in 721, the city fell.

Ultimately, then, Isaiah ben Amoz's prediction of Israel's demise was proven right: within two decades Samaria had been destroyed, its people deported, and the territory turned into an Assyrian province. (The perceived fulfilment of this and other oracles is doubtless one of the reasons that the Isaiah traditions were first preserved; as Deut 18:22 reflects, true prophecies were recognized after the fact.) Isaiah ben Amoz's response to these events is essentially in keeping with his earlier advice to Ahaz: reliance on humans rather than YHWH is futile. Reflecting on the northern kingdom's demise, Isaiah ben Amoz comments:

> The Lord sent a word against Jacob,
>   and it fell on Israel;
> and all the people knew it –
>   Ephraim and the inhabitants of Samaria –
>   but in pride and arrogance of heart they said:
> 'The bricks have fallen,
>   but we will build with dressed stones;
> the sycamores have been cut down,
>   but we will put cedars in their place.'
> So YHWH raised adversaries against them,
>   and stirred up their enemies. (9:8–11)

Samaria's defeat was due to its failure to trust in YHWH; rather than being chastened and warned by its earlier mishaps, it foolishly persisted in relying on its own power and on political alliances instead.

A decade after Samaria's fall, Isaiah ben Amoz's advice continued in much the same vein, as Judah considered joining in a series of anti-Assyrian rebellions among the Philistine city-states. Like the northern kingdom, the Philistines had allied themselves with Egypt. Judah's kings were clearly tempted to join in, believing that between the smaller kingdoms' efforts and the greater power of the Egyptian military they might succeed in their efforts to throw off Assyrian authority. Isaiah ben Amoz's message, again, is that they should not rely on such alliances: foreign kings are unreliable, and the consequences of rebellion will be dire.

There appears to be a fair amount of material in the book of Isaiah that relates to this turmoil, including an oracle from 715 warning the Philistines that their rejoicing would prove immature (14:28–32) because the Assyrian army was coming 'out of the north' to crush the rebellion (14:31). (Mesopotamian armies heading west followed the curve of the Fertile Crescent, up along the Euphrates and then down along the Levantine coast, so that from the Levantine perspective they came from the north; compare Jer 4:6; 6:1; 10:22; 50:41 etc.) The end of the oracle warns the political negotiators in Jerusalem against the foreign envoys who seek their cooperation in rebellion: Zion is YHWH's city, and YHWH alone is necessary to defend it (14:32).

Egypt's important role in the geopolitics of this period will by now be clear. The oracles against the Nile kingdoms in Isa 18–19 and the sign-act of Isa 20, in which Isaiah ben Amoz wanders around Jerusalem naked to signify the defeat of Egypt by the Assyrians, are also from this time. The oracle in Isa 18, like the one against the Philistines in Isa 14, warns against political and military alliances, referring to the Cushite ambassadors sent into the Levant in search of support (18:1–2). At stake in these passages, as with many prophetic oracles concerning foreign nations, is YHWH's status as supreme deity. Divine foreknowledge is invoked as evidence that YHWH and YHWH alone is in control of world events: 'Where now are your sages?', asks Isaiah ben Amoz; 'Let them tell you and make known what YHWH of hosts has planned against Egypt!' (19:12). Divine foreknowledge as evidence of YHWH's power will also be a prominent feature of Second Isaiah's arguments.

The sign-act in Isa 20 is dated to 711, towards the end of a decade of Philistine rebellion. Again, the focus is on Egypt, not Philistia, with an emphasis on Egyptian unreliability that is strongly characteristic of the eighth- and later seventh-century Isaiah traditions. In the retrospective narrative of Isa 36, for example, the Rabshekah who taunts Judah's officials orders them to

> Say to Hezekiah: Thus says the great king, the king of Assyria: On what do you base this confidence of yours? Do you think that mere words are strategy and power for war? On whom do you now rely, that you have rebelled against me? See, you are relying on Egypt, that broken reed of a staff, which will pierce the hand of anyone who leans on it. Such is Pharaoh king of Egypt to all who rely on him. (36:4–6)

Hindsight, of course, is 20/20. Egypt would, on more than one occasion, prove itself the kind of ally who could not be counted on to appear when needed. Even though Egypt's significance tends to be overshadowed by Assyria and later Babylonia, it was a key player in Levantine politics for several centuries. Ultimately, reliance on Egypt in rebellions against the Mesopotamian empires would be a critical factor in Judah's demise.

Contemporary with events in the late eighth century is Isa 28, which depicts a drunken ritual in which Judah's religious and political leaders cement a treaty with Egypt. The prophecy plays on the similarity in sound between the name of the Egyptian goddess Mut (*mwt*) and the Hebrew word for death (also *mwt*). This alliance with Egypt, Isaiah ben Amoz warns, is 'a covenant with death' (28:15; Hays). Egypt may be fun to party with, and it may talk a good game – but when push comes to shove, its armies will not help Judah. Again, the people are urged to trust in YHWH: 'One who trusts will not panic' (28:16). The kingdom's leaders' trust in Egypt is misplaced; as a consequence, the flood – a term signalling impending cosmic disaster, and in this case specifically the overpowering Assyrian military might (compare 8:8) – will overwhelm them (28:17–19).

Isaiah ben Amoz's conviction that even the mighty Assyrian kings were under YHWH's command is even more explicit elsewhere; the empire is described as the 'rod of [YHWH's] anger', with even the weapons they wield extensions of YHWH's own wrath (10:5). Horrific though the prospect may be, it is YHWH himself who sends the empire to terrify the people (10:6; note the 'strange deed' and 'alien work' in 28:21). However, Assyria's excess in carrying out this commission, and its arrogance in claiming that it was done under its own authority, is subsequently punished (10:12–19). This description of the empire's demise was perhaps made explicit as part of the book's development in the seventh century, as Assyrian power was waning and YHWH's primacy was emphasized under Josiah. That such hopes were fostered already in the eighth century, however, is signalled by the glee of Isa 14, which almost certainly originally rejoiced over Sargon II's ignominious death on the battlefield:

> All the kings of the nations lie in glory,
>> each in his own tomb;
> but you are cast out, away from your grave,
>> like loathsome carrion,
> clothed with the dead, those pierced by the sword,
>> who go down to the stones of the Pit,
>> like a corpse trampled underfoot.
> You will not be joined with them in burial,
>> because you have destroyed your land,
>> you have killed your people. (14:18–20)

Many centuries later, Milton's portrait of the fall of Satan in *Paradise Lost* would also owe something to Isa 14's description of the fall of the Assyrian king.

Against a background of fevered international politics, Isaiah ben Amoz thus persistently advocates a policy of 'rest and repose' (28:12), in contrast to a frenzy of military activity driven by fear. As noted above, Isaiah ben Amoz's advice to this effect could also be politically savvy: Ahaz ought to have remained calm and let the Assyrians deal with Rezin and Pekah themselves, rather than letting his fear get the better of him and ensuring Assyrian support by becoming an Assyrian vassal.

Nevertheless, Isaiah ben Amoz's advice does not seem to have been motivated by *Realpolitik*. In the midst of Sennacherib's siege of Jerusalem in 701, for example, Isaiah ben Amoz condemned King Hezekiah because 'You counted the houses of Jerusalem, and you broke down the houses to fortify the wall' (22:10). Militarily, fortifying the wall made perfect sense – at the cost of a few houses, Hezekiah was better able to protect the city from Sennacherib and his army. But Isaiah ben Amoz objected to Hezekiah's actions: firstly, because they signified a fear of the enemy rather than a trust in YHWH's protection and, secondly, because they constituted another instance of power abuse, in which royal authority was used to evict poorer and more vulnerable citizens from their homes.

In First Isaiah as it now stands, the survival of Jerusalem in 701 is arguably the central historical and theological event. Isaiah ben Amoz had predicted that YHWH would protect the city, promising that

> YHWH of hosts will come down
> to fight upon Mount Zion and upon its hill.
> Like birds hovering overhead, so YHWH of hosts
> will protect Jerusalem;
> he will protect and deliver it,
> he will spare and rescue it. (31:4–5)

For the eventual editors of the book, the siege of 701 brought into focus much of Isaiah's message: YHWH alone holds the power to protect the people. The two versions of the city's deliverance preserved in Isaiah's narrative account of 701 both emphasize the centrality of YHWH's divine protection: the version that attributes Jerusalem's survival to YHWH provoking rumours of rebellions elsewhere, prompting Sennacherib to move on (37:7), and the version in which YHWH sends an angel into the Assyrian camp and kills 185,000 Assyrian soldiers (37:36). Though probably borrowed from the

Deuteronomistic narrative of Judah's history in 2 Kings, these accounts are in keeping with Isaiah ben Amoz's emphasis on the importance of Judah's reliance on Yhwh, rather than on military power or political machinations.

Implicitly or explicitly, Isaiah ben Amoz's advice to Judah's kings is motivated by the idea that Yhwh is specially attached to the city of Jerusalem and its temple. A century later, the expectation that Yhwh would therefore protect Zion against invaders came to a shocking end, as the king of Babylon and his army breached the walls of Jerusalem and burned down the city – including Yhwh's temple. The Isaianic editors of the book of Isaiah sought to explain the unthinkable by inserting a story blaming Hezekiah for showing Babylonian emissaries too much of the nation's wealth, and thus tempting them to conquer Jerusalem (Isa 39). Beyond this, the book almost completely avoids talking about the downfall of Judah. When the story resumes in Isa 40, it is already looking back at the exile.

There are, however, a number of important texts in the book of Isaiah that stem from the intervening years; to these this guide now turns.

Further reading

Aster, Shawn Zelig. *Reflections of Empire in Isaiah 1–39: Responses to Assyrian Ideology*. Atlanta, GA: Society of Biblical Literature, 2017.

Coomber, Matthew J. M. *Re-Reading the Prophets through Corporate Globalization: A Cultural-Evolutionary Approach to Economic Injustice in the Hebrew Bible*. Piscataway, NJ: Gorgias, 2010.

Couey, J. Blake. *Reading the Poetry of First Isaiah: The Most Perfect Model of the Prophetic Poetry*. Oxford: Oxford University Press, 2015.

Hays, Christopher B. *A Covenant with Death: Death in the Iron Age II and Its Rhetorical Uses in Proto-Isaiah*. Grand Rapids, MI: Eerdmans, 2015.

de Jong, Matthijs J. *Isaiah among the Ancient Near Eastern Prophets: A Comparative Study of the Earliest Stages of the Isaiah Tradition and the Neo-Assyrian Prophecies*. Leiden: Brill, 2007.

Young, Robb A. *Hezekiah in History and Tradition*. Leiden: Brill, 2012.

2

Isaiah in the seventh century

One of the more controversial aspects of the book of Isaiah's formation concerns the century and a half between its origins with Isaiah ben Amoz in the late eighth century and the mid- to late sixth century, when it was picked up and significantly expanded by an anonymous prophet to the Babylonian exiles. Although not yet as widely acknowledged as the eighth-, sixth-, and fifth-century stages of the book's development, a number of scholars have drawn attention to signs that a version of the book developed by Isaiah ben Amoz and his immediate disciples was significantly revised in the late seventh century. These revisions are plausibly linked to the collapse of the Neo-Assyrian Empire, whose expansionist policies had formed the backdrop of Isaiah ben Amoz's earlier work, and to growing hope that Judah might regain its full political independence in the wake of Assyria's demise.

The leader upon whom this hope was pinned is not named, but other biblical texts suggest a significant degree of intellectual, religious, and political ferment around King Josiah (r. 640–609). Unfortunately, both the circumstances and the precise extent of a Josianic edition of the book of Isaiah have been largely obscured, because the dream that Judah might escape foreign domination was ultimately dashed by Josiah's untimely death and the rise of the Neo-Babylonian Empire. What survives contains sketches of an idealized king, whose just and righteous rule is supported by Yhwh, in a kingdom free of foreign interference.

Historical context

Though the late eighth century was marked by various Levantine efforts to throw off Assyrian dominance, the seventh century was characterized by the widespread realization that political and military resistance to the Assyrian behemoth was largely futile. After Hezekiah's submission to Sennacherib in

701, Judah's kings did not rebel against the Assyrian Empire again. Manasseh (r. 687–642) is depicted in the Assyrian annals as a loyal vassal, sending supplies for Esarhaddon's (r. 680–669) new palace at Nineveh and troops to support Assurbanipal's (r. 668–627) campaign against rebels in Egypt. They give no sign that he ever tried to revolt against his imperial suzerain. Only Chronicles claims that Judah was anything other than a docile vassal state during this period, but the curious story of the Assyrians taking Manasseh in manacles to Babylon is almost certainly an anachronistic attempt to explain his lengthy reign in the terms of its strict theology of retribution (2 Chr 33). In political terms, Manasseh's reign is explicable as a result of unwavering submission to Assyrian power. Unlike Hezekiah or the leaders of the former northern kingdom, the Assyrians had no reason to unseat this loyal vassal from his throne in Jerusalem. Biblical writers turned this lack of overt interference to their theological and ideological advantage, maintaining a near-complete silence concerning the presence of foreign powers in the region that bolstered the literary illusion of an autonomous Judah.

Although these texts obscure the empire's significance, Assyria remained the most important single factor affecting Judah's political, economic and social existence in the seventh century. The phrase *pax Assyriaca* ('Assyrian peace') is used to describe the stabilization of relationships between Assyria and its western vassals during this period, together with the associated reduction in political and military tumult. As the majority of the Levant came under Assyrian control, conflict among vassal states was discouraged; outright rebellion was dealt with as quickly as possible. Assyrian control was largely solidified by the turn of the century and Assyrian military activity in the region reduced dramatically thereafter: in the sixty years after 705, there were only three western campaigns of any magnitude. The empire's grasp on the region created a sphere of influence in which concerns about political subordination could largely give way to other matters. Despite occasional rumbling (usually in conjunction with the death of an Assyrian king), the upper hand was clearly Assyrian.

The Assyrians established a number of settlements in the Levant as part of their network of military, economic and administrative control. One important centre may have been at Ramat Rahel, a few kilometres south of Jerusalem. Just out of sight of the City of David, the site appears to have been used by imperial governors, and perhaps their associated military detachments, to keep an eye on the king in Jerusalem. Radiating out from such centres, imperial influence extended to most aspects of Judahite life, from national political policy down to the material goods used in the home. The Assyrians encouraged regional economic development, including industrial oil production in the Shephelah (the transitional hill country in south-central Judah between the mountains and the coastal plain). They also exploited the results of such support via tribute payments and trade. As in the eighth century, the weight of these payments could be crushing.

After more than a century of influence and more than seventy-five years of undisputed power, Assyrian dominance of the Levant finally cracked in the last third of the seventh century – from the Levantine perspective, almost completely without warning. Although the exact reasons for the empire's collapse remain opaque, it is widely suspected that it was a result of two main factors. First, Assyria was plagued in its last years by a succession of ineffective kings, whose personal weaknesses were exacerbated by their relatively brief tenure. The death of Assurbanipal in 627 is usually identified as a crucial turning point; whereas he and his predecessor Esarhaddon had effectively consolidated and extended imperial control, none of his successors proved to be capable of leading the sprawling empire effectively.

Second – and to be fair to those last Assyrian kings – the greatest empire the world had ever known had probably finally overreached itself. In theory, the mighty Assyrian Empire sprawled from its Mesopotamian heartland in all directions: eastward to Media, southward to Elam and Babylonia, northward to Urartu, westward to the Levant, and to Egypt in the far southwest. In reality, its grip on the outer reaches of this empire had always been tenuous. Protracted efforts to assert control over Egypt proved especially costly; a brief period of control in the middle of the seventh century required multiple campaigns and the support of numerous allies and vassals. Egypt's subsequent re-assertions of autonomy included increasing interference in the southern Levant; as in the previous century, Egypt would be a key outside factor in Judahite politics as the kingdom approached its final demise.

Nearer to home, Babylonia – a long-standing thorn in Assyria's southern flank – began in the 620s to rise up against Assyrian imperial authority. It has been theorized that the major cities of the Assyrian heartland, so far from the empire frontiers, were insufficiently fortified against an attack from so close at hand. At some point, Assyria was forced to abandon its distant territories, withdrawing its armies from the southern Levant and elsewhere in an attempt to defend the Assyrian homeland against these Babylonian attacks. Despite these defensive efforts, the Assyrian capital at Nineveh fell to Babylonian troops in 612.

Awareness of Assyria's growing vulnerability was likely responsible for several rebellions in the western territories around this time. By 609, the Babylonian army had destroyed a coalition of Assyrian and Egyptian troops seeking to defend this territory against Babylonian incursions. In due course, the Babylonian Empire would assume control of all of Assyria's territories – claiming for itself the riches and rewards of its far-flung provinces and vassal kingdoms, then using them as stepping stones to even wider powers.

The traditional narrative of this period has portrayed the Assyrians' departure from the southern Levant as producing a complete power vacuum, into which the Judahite king Josiah stepped unopposed: first purging the temple of Assyrian elements, then campaigning into the former northern kingdom in an attempt to re-establish a grand, Davidic kingdom (2 Kgs 22–23).

Both Kings and Chronicles report that Josiah was only eight years old when he ascended the throne after the assassination of his father Amon. The Assyrian Empire began its downward spiral just as Josiah reached adulthood; the Chronicler dates the beginning of Josiah's 'reforms' to the twelfth year of his reign, when he was about twenty years old (2 Chr 34:3). This would have been 627, the same year that Assurbanipal died. The Chronicler, who notes that Josiah's religious interest began 'while he was still a boy', may have had an interest in dating the reforms as early in his reign as possible; 2 Kgs 22 dates the beginning of the reforms slightly later, to Josiah's eighteenth regnal year, 621. The exact date is incidental to the broader coincidence of events: just as the boy-king came of age, the once-invincible Assyrian Empire started to show signs of weakness.

If the political environment was turbulent, it was also promising, and it would surely have been natural to focus the kingdom's hopes on its young, energetic king (Sweeney). The extremely positive assessment offered by the Deuteronomistic Historian – 'before him there was no king like him, who turned to Yhwh with all his heart, with all his soul, and with all his might, according to all the law of Moses; nor did any like him arise after him' (2 Kgs 23:25) – has suggested to many scholars that a version of the Deuteronomistic History (Deuteronomy–2 Kings) was written during his reign, arising from and contributing to this enthusiastic atmosphere.

The nature and extent of the reforms that the Deuteronomistic History attributes to Josiah (2 Kgs 23:1–27) has been intensely debated. They have long been considered a watershed moment in the history and religion of Israel, connected to the Deuteronomistic movement and its emphasis on worship centralized in Jerusalem and the worship of Yhwh alone – a crucial stage in the development of Israelite monotheism. But the reforms are mentioned only in 2 Kgs 22–23 (and the parallel text in 2 Chr 34–35, but the two texts disagree on key points). They go unremarked in biblical texts written just a few years later, including the ones that exhibit Deuteronomistic influences. Especially striking is that they are not mentioned in the book of Jeremiah, even though that prophet is supposed to have been active during Josiah's reign (Jer 1:2), and the book itself exhibits many affinities with deuteronomistic thought. Nor are there signs of destruction at religious sites outside of Jerusalem, such as might support the biblical text's claim that Josiah destroyed the 'high places' outside the city (2 Kgs 23:4, 15–20). One of the few signs of change in the material culture is a decrease in astral motifs in the iconographic record – perhaps a sign of waning Assyrian influence.

The collapse of the Assyrian Empire probably did result in a clear-out of certain items from the Jerusalem temple. There had surely been a significant amount of 'elite emulation', in which some Judahites may have been drawn to worship Assyrian deities because they were associated with the people and empire in power – an interest reflected in 2 Kgs 16's story of King Ahaz adopting an altar style that he saw in Damascus. The Assyrians did not impose their religion on vassals, but they did make their presence felt, even in the sanctuaries of client states. The recent discovery of an Assyrian treaty-tablet that had been hung in the inner sanctum of an Iron Age temple in Tel Tayinat, Syria, illustrates the sort of symbolic weight of Assyrian rule. The Assyrians' withdrawal from the region would thus have been a natural moment to remove any associated items from Judah's principal sanctuary. It is possible, though not certain, that this process included renewed assertions regarding the superiority of the kingdom's native deity, Yʜwʜ.

At the same time, there is increasingly compelling archaeological evidence that the Egyptians had control of the southern coast of the Levant for a short period at the end of the seventh century. Though there are no written sources that would clarify the nature or extent of this authority, there are numerous signs of increased Egyptian influence in the region, including an increase in both the quantity and quality of Egyptian artefacts. These and other signs suggest that the Egyptians had effectively succeeded the Assyrians as the dominant foreign power in the area, collecting tithes and tributes and dictating regional policy. Although Judah does not appear to have come under direct Egyptian control, changes in its weight system and other aspects of life suggest heightened sensitivity to Egyptian power – and, significantly, an inclination to work within rather than against it. Although some within Judah may have dreamed of a grand Josianic kingdom, completely free of external influence, a pragmatic assessment of the political situation would have recognized that such ambitions were unlikely to be fully realized.

The peak of this Egyptian influence in the Levant appears to have been between about 616 and 605. It is probably significant, therefore, that Josiah died by the hand of the Egyptian Pharaoh Necho II in 609, at the height of Egyptian power. Josiah's death has traditionally been attributed to a failed attempt to prevent Necho from supporting the Assyrians against the Babylonians, with the meeting at Megiddo (recounted, very briefly, in 2 Kgs 23:29) interpreted as an overtly military confrontation. More recently, it has been suggested that Josiah had come to Megiddo to register his allegiance to Egypt, but was suspected of disloyalty and executed.

Whatever the exact reason for Josiah's death, the extent of Egypt's involvement in Judahite politics at the end of the seventh century is clear from its subsequent interference in the succession of Judah's kingship. Though one of Josiah's sons, Shallum (r. 609, throne name Jehoahaz), initially succeeded him on the throne, he reigned for just a few months before Necho deposed him in favour of his brother, Eliakim (r. 609–598, throne name Jehoiakim). Both Jeremiah and Ezekiel refer briefly to this episode (Jer 22:11–12; Ezek 19:4).

The final years of the seventh century and first decades of the sixth would underscore the futility of any attempt to extricate Judah from foreign rule. The battle between Egypt and Babylonia for control over the Levant eventually gave Babylon the upper hand; two failed rebellions against Babylonian authority led to Jerusalem's destruction in 586 and the kingdom's transformation into a province under direct Babylonian rule.

Josiah's embarrassing and untimely death, followed so quickly by Jerusalem's twofold defeat (597, 586) must have left people wondering how the kingdom's affairs had gone so wrong, so quickly. Whatever dreams of independence Judah might have fostered under Josiah had been finally and firmly quashed. The extant Deuteronomistic History is probably an attempt to explain why the kingdom had fallen, despite Josiah's greatness (2 Kgs 23:26–27).

Theological themes and concerns

A number of key passages in First Isaiah (Isa 1–39) have been linked to hopes surrounding the collapse of the Assyrian Empire and the reign of Josiah. These passages reiterate YHWH's lordship over the nations, in particular the Assyrians, and are full of excitement at the prospect of a king whose exemplary reign would fill the kingdom and beyond with justice and righteousness. The anonymity of this king in the surviving tradition is likely a consequence of Josiah's premature death. Josiah's demise, followed rapidly by the kingdom's surrender to first Egyptian and then Babylonian dominance, dashed the hopes for national autonomy that had sprung up in response to waning Assyrian power. In the face of these events, Isaianic dreams of freedom from foreign oppression pivoted towards a future messiah, whose identity remained unknown.

Unlike the revision associated with the sixth century, the changes thought to have been made in the seventh century do not constitute a lengthy, multi-chapter addition, readily differentiable from the older material. Rather, this stage of development involved a series of shorter annotations, none more than a chapter in length. This is one of the reasons that the existence of a seventh-century version of Isaiah is contested: the material it is thought to include is interspersed with the eighth-century material, rather than comprising a clearly distinct section. The proposed seventh-century passages elaborate on the older Isaianic traditions, explaining their significance for the current generation. They emphasize that Yнwн's punishment of Judah at Assyria's hand is now coming to an end and that the end of Assyrian rule will enable a new golden age, in which the kingdom is led by a native king who has been gifted by Yнwн with royal attributes ideal for the purpose.

The identification of this material is further complicated by its anonymity; if Josiah was ever explicitly named as the king in whom the kingdom had invested these hopes, his name has been obscured in the wake of his failure. Many of these passages were then taken up in later generations as descriptions of a future messiah, whose coming would inaugurate an era of perfect justice and righteousness. ('Messiah' means 'anointed' and was once a common way of referring to Israel and Judah's kings, who were anointed as part of their coronation; for example, 1 Sam 2:10; 24:6; Pss 2:2; 18:50.)

Expressions of expectation regarding this idealized king are concentrated especially in Isa 9; 11; and 32. In the first half of Isa 9, the blindness for which Isaiah ben Amoz castigated the kingdom and its rulers, warning of the punishment Yнwн would wreak upon them for their unwillingness to amend their ways, is at last given a solution (9:2, cf. 6:9–10). The kingdom's transformation is linked specifically to the birth of a royal child (9:6), under whose authority the yoke of Assyrian oppression will finally be broken (9:4–5; the 'yoke of Assur' was the standard Assyrian phrase for the imposition of its imperial authority). Justice and righteousness – previously so elusive that Isaiah ben Amoz made them a cornerstone of his message (e.g. 5:7, 16; 28:17) – will finally be established (9:7; cf. 16:4b–5).

It is possible that one of Isaiah ben Amoz's oracles, with another royal son in mind, has been here understood as applying also (or instead) to Josiah, although the youth of the one in whom these hopes are placed has tended in most interpreters' eyes to favour Josiah. Josiah was only eight years old when he came to the throne after the assassination of his father Amon. Hezekiah, the other Judahite king viewed favourably within the book, was already 25 at his accession. The complex set of royal titles in Isa 9:6 may also have Egyptian parallels – pharaohs had five different names – which would make sense in the context of an Egyptian resurgence in the mid-seventh century.

The youth of the king is especially emphasized by Isa 11:6 ('a little child shall lead them'). The imagery suggests a boy-king (a 'shoot', 11:1) whose reign was endangered by the demise of his predecessor (the 'stump'). Whereas Manasseh's father Hezekiah died apparently of old age (2 Kgs 20:21), Josiah's father Amon was killed in a palace coup, putting the dynastic line in danger (2 Kgs 21:23–24).

In any case, Josiah's eventual failure to fulfil the expectations placed on him appears to have led to a more generic interpretation: instead of addressing the kingdom's flourishing in the current king's reign, these verses came to be understood as anticipating the coming of a future messiah. It is in this sense that this and other materials originally composed with reference to Josiah were picked up and used by the early Christian community to interpret the significance of Jesus of Nazareth, whom they identified as Israel's long-awaited messiah (e.g. Rom 15; 2 Cor 4; Rev 19). Early rabbinic interpretations also read much of this material messianically, although usually with reference to Hezekiah, or to Hezekiah as a model for a messiah yet to appear (b. Sanh. 94a; Rab. Ruth 7:2; Rab. Gen. 97). The vision of all creation living peaceably together (11:6–9) remains one of the most common images of the messianic age, in both Jewish and Christian traditions.

Isaiah 11, like Isa 9:2–7, picks up the key Isaianic terminology of justice and righteousness to emphasize the transformative capacity of this era:

> with righteousness he shall judge the poor,
>   and decide with equity for the meek of the earth;
> he shall strike the earth with the rod of his mouth,
>   and with the breath of his lips he shall kill the wicked.
> Righteousness shall be the belt around his waist,
>   and faithfulness the belt around his loins. (11:4–5)

This vocabulary is similarly prominent in Isa 32, which looks forward to a king who will 'reign in righteousness' and princes who will 'rule with justice' (32:1). These oracles mirror the royal attributes for which the psalmist pleads with YHWH: 'Give the king your justice, O God, and your righteousness to a king's son; May he judge your people with righteousness, and your poor with justice' (Ps 72:1–2).

Both traditions are in line with classic ancient Near Eastern ideals: the well-being of a kingdom was perceived to be largely dependent upon its king's commitment to just government on the gods' behalf. In keeping with this theological perspective, Isaiah 11 and other passages associated with the seventh-century version of the book attribute its king's just and righteous reign to his faithful trust in YHWH (7:9; 16:5; 25:1; 26:2; cf. 28:16–17). Throughout the Isaianic traditions, the pursuit of justice and righteousness is a crucial means by which both king and people show their commitment to YHWH.

Isaiah 32 also exuberantly reverses the Isaianic depiction of the people as blind and deaf, declaring that under the new king even the blind will see and the deaf will hear (32:3–4, cf. 6:9–10). Those who have known the upheaval and instability of the kingdom under other rulers, who were incapable (or unwilling) to trust in YHWH and enact justice, will finally find rest (32:16–18). The active pursuit of justice and a commitment to righteousness are crucial to this idyllic vision; well-being and restful quiet are possible only as a result of the establishment of justice and righteousness in the kingdom (32:17–18).

The chapter speaks also of the desertion of a fortified palace on a hill, referring perhaps to the Assyrian administrative centre at Ramat Rahel. The site was abandoned as the Assyrians retreated from the Levant; their absence makes room for justice and righteousness in the kingdom (32:14–16; cf. 33:18–20). This vision of a revitalized native monarchy ill-suits a date after the kingdom's destruction; by contrast, other biblical traditions express only limited hope for a restoration of the Davidic monarchy after the sixth century. It is also clearly at odds with Second and Third Isaiah's visions of restoration, where only YHWH is king. Within the book of Isaiah, then, these hopes seem to have their origins at a time when Jerusalem still stood as the capital of an independent kingdom – when the inviolability of Zion that had been suggested by its survival against the Assyrians in Isaiah ben Amoz's time had yet to be shattered. These chapters may once have stood at the end of the seventh-century version of the book.

As already intimated, this seventh-century revision of the Isaianic traditions made significant use of the eighth-century traditions it had inherited, as it sought to re-interpret and re-apply Isaiah ben Amoz's words to the later context. This re-use is especially visible in the oracles against the nations, which appear mainly in Isa 13–23. In the final form of the book, these oracles begin with an oracle targeting Babylon and clearly presuppose both the rise and eventual fall of that empire. It is equally clear that they contain a substantial amount of older material, especially insofar as much of it presumes eighth-century Levantine political realities.

Some of this material appears to have been annotated from a seventh-century perspective, as an editor (or editors) sought to signal the ongoing significance of Isaiah ben Amoz's prophecies for his (or her, but more likely his) own day. The oracular material concerning Moab (Isa 15–16), for example, seems mainly to presuppose circumstances in the eighth century; the depiction of the Moabites as distressed birds echoes both earlier material concerning the Assyrians in Isaiah (10:14) and Assyrian descriptions of their attacks on enemy cities (recall Hezekiah, shut up in Jerusalem 'like a bird in a cage'). Moab was finally destroyed in 582 by the Babylonians; this being well after Jerusalem would have provided a place of refuge (16:1–4), the main body of the oracle certainly pre-dates the sixth century. That it does so by some decades is indicated most explicitly in the final verses, which describe the preceding material as 'what Yʜwʜ spoke concerning Moab in the past' (16:13). Someone has then updated the oracle, warning that Moab will be humbled within just three years (16:14). It is difficult to date such a warning with any precision, but other small additions in these oracles concerning the nations indicate work in the late seventh century.

An oracle originally concerned with the fate of the coastal city of Tyre, when it was besieged by the Assyrian king Sennacherib in his western campaign at the end of the eighth century – the same campaign that saw Jerusalem just barely escape, and in the context of which Isaiah of Jerusalem warned extensively about relying on Egypt for help (cf. 23:5) – also seems to have been reworked initially in the late seventh century, in anticipation of Tyre's renewed autonomy as the Assyrians left the region (23:15–18). It was revised again in light of the thirteen-year siege and eventual destruction of the city by the Babylonians (586–573, Isa 23:13–14).

Similarly, the oracle now cast as concerning the Babylonian king (14:3–27) is widely thought to have originated as an eighth-century oracle concerning the Assyrian king Sargon II, celebrating his death on the battlefield in 705. Although the extant form of the text gives no explicit sign that it was re-envisioned already in the seventh century to speak more generally of the downfall of the Assyrian Empire, the final verses (14:24–27) echo sentiments found in Isa 10:5–19, where an older oracle concerning Yʜᴡʜ's use of Assyria as a punitive rod against Israel and Judah has been annotated to warn of Assyria's coming demise. A similar declaration of coming judgement on Assyria appears at the end of Isa 30, updating older Isaianic material in anticipation of the empire's end (30:18–33). Assyria's crime is hubris: Yʜᴡʜ chose to use the empire for his own ends, but the 'plan that is planned concerning the whole earth' is Yʜᴡʜ's alone (14:26; cf. 10:15). Assyria made the mistake of thinking that its power was its own. This error must be exposed and the true power of Yʜᴡʜ acknowledged; therefore Assyria must fall. Isaiah ben Amoz's depiction of Yʜᴡʜ as God of all the earth, able to command foreign kings and armies to do his bidding, is thus reiterated by a seventh-century edition that views Assyria's imminent downfall as affirmative evidence that Yʜᴡʜ was in control all along.

Isaiah 24–27 forms a capstone to the litany of oracles concerning the nations. Rather than taking aim at a single foreign adversary, these chapters speak in sweeping terms of Yʜᴡʜ's global authority, affirming Yʜᴡʜ's control over all kingdoms and countries (24:1; 25:9). They assert that the land's domination by the Assyrians resulted from the failure to keep the laws and statutes of the covenant (24:5), just as Josiah emphasized (2 Kgs 23:3) after finding the book of the law (2 Kgs 22:10–13); the people's disobedience has resulted in the land being cursed (Isa 24:6; cf. Deut 29:20).

Albeit with one eye on the past, these chapters also look forward to a new age of Judahite independence (Hays). Other 'lords' – that is, foreign kings – may have seemed to rule over Judah, but the people are now encouraged to acknowledge Yʜᴡʜ alone (26:13; compare the importance of Yʜᴡʜ-alone worship in 2 Kgs 23:4–14; Deut 6:4–5; 12). The citadel whose destruction is celebrated may be the imperial centre at Ramat Rahel, the 'city of foreigners' from which Assyrian troops were withdrawn sometime in the 620s (24:10; 25:2; cf. 32:9–14). Deliverance from imperial power is imagined as a national revivification from a state of death (26:19; as earlier in Hos 6, later Ezek 37, and commonly in ancient Near Eastern rhetoric). A luxurious feast on the Temple Mount to celebrate this divine victory is announced in Isa 25:6–8. There may also be expressions of aspirations for renewed influence over regions long lost to Judahite control (Isa 25–26, e.g. 26:15), including the reintegration of the peoples of the former northern kingdom into the worship of YHWH at Jerusalem (27:5). No *asherim*, 'sacred poles', altars on the high places, or other idolatrous objects may remain (27:9; 30:22; cf. Deut 7:5, 25; 12:3; 2 Kgs 23:6).

In past scholarship, Isa 24–27 was sometimes dated to Hellenistic times and called an 'apocalypse', which categorized it with the latest literature in the Hebrew Bible, such as Daniel. Although some of its themes, including widespread devastation of the land, divine rule, and the dead rising, resonate with apocalyptic themes, on the whole this theory is not tenable. The genre of Isa 24–27 is not that of an apocalypse, and all of its themes are characteristic of earlier literature as well. Furthermore, its Hebrew language does not show the marks of lateness that are found so clearly in Daniel and other late postexilic Hebrew literature. Thus the theory of a Hellenistic date for Isa 24–27 has increasingly fallen by the wayside.

Finally (and as noted in the previous chapter), it is possible that a version of Isa 36–37 may have been written around this time. Because these chapters closely parallel 1 Kgs 18:13–19:37, however, it may be that they originated as part of the Deuteronomistic History, only later to make their way into the book of Isaiah. The reverse has also been argued: that these chapters originated in Isaiah, and were taken over by the editors of Kings. (For a survey and discussion, see Kahn.)

In the final form of the book, this second, seventh-century edition of the book of Isaiah has been somewhat submerged under later sixth- and fifth-century additions. Indeed, it is also likely that some of the specificity that once characterized these passages has been deliberately obscured, after the dreams they represent were foiled by the rising power of Egypt and Babylonia and by Josiah's sudden death in 609. In much the same way, after the shocking death of Assyria's Sargon II on the battlefield, he was de-emphasized by the scribes of his successor, Sennacherib. This could be viewed as a milder form of the *damnatio memoriae* ('condemnation of memory') to which pharaohs often subjected their predecessors. The second half of Isa 27:11, for example, sounds a bit like a frustrated editor, annotating these hopeful texts in the wake of Josiah's death in an attempt to explain why they have not come to pass: 'this is a people without understanding; therefore, he that made them [that is, YHWH] will not have compassion on them, he that formed them will show them no favour'. Because the people have failed to understand what they have been told, YHWH has abandoned them to their fate at the hands of the next generation of empires.

Further reading

Hays, Christopher B. *The Origins of Isaiah 24–27: Josiah's Festival Scroll for the Fall of Assyria*. Cambridge: Cambridge University Press, 2019.

Hibbard, James Todd, and Hyun Chul Paul Kim, eds. *Formation and Intertextuality in Isaiah 24–27*. Ancient Israel and Its Literature 17. Atlanta, GA: Society of Biblical Literature, 2013.

Kahn, Dan'el. *Sennacherib's Campaign against Judah: A Source Analysis of Isaiah 36–37*. Cambridge: Cambridge University Press, 2020.

Sweeney, Marvin A. *King Josiah of Judah: The Lost Messiah of Israel*. Oxford: Oxford University Press, 2001.

3

Isaiah in the sixth century

Starting with Isa 40, the reader is quite suddenly in a new context – sometime in the 530s, about 150 years after the career of Isaiah ben Amoz and seventy years after the time of Josiah. Jerusalem and the Temple had been destroyed by the Babylonians in 586, and many of the people deported to Babylonia, where by this time they and their descendants had been living for half a century.

It is universally agreed among serious scholars that nothing after Isa 40 stems from the time of Isaiah ben Amoz. Although this idea would not emerge in academic scholarship until the late eighteenth century, the medieval Jewish commentator Abraham Ibn Ezra was already questioning whether Isa 40–66 could have been authored by Isaiah ben Amoz. Indeed, the chapters themselves do not claim that they are: whereas Isaiah's name occurs sixteen times in Isa 1–39, including three editorial headings that explicitly assert Isaianic authorship (1:1; 2:1; 13:1), the prophet from whom the book takes its name is absent from the subsequent material. The chapters from Isa 40 onwards thus do not appear to be making any overt claim to Isaianic authorship, even as they are appended to the older Isaianic traditions.

The means by which the book of Isaiah was preserved and transmitted from the late seventh century to the late sixth century is something of a mystery. Indeed, one of the most recent disputes in Isaiah scholarship is whether the book's development in the Babylonian period took place among the deportees and their descendants in Babylonia, among those in provincial Judah, or a combination of both. The material joined to the book from this period is, as noted in the Introduction, commonly referred to as Second Isaiah, in recognition of the significant historical and authorial break between these and the preceding chapters, and in the absence of a named prophet to which they are attributed.

Historical context

In the 530s, the once indomitable Babylonian Empire came to a sudden and unexpected end. Cyrus of Persia defeated the Babylonians in 539, and his imperial machine quickly swallowed up the sprawling Babylonian territories. The new Persian Empire then pressed on into Egypt, India and Macedonia, reaching its full extent within just a few decades. At the time, its success was not a foregone conclusion. Cyrus's reign (r. 559–530) lasted less than a decade after his conquest of Babylon and his son, Cambyses II (r. 530–522), died on his way back from an expedition to Egypt after a mere eight years on the throne. Another son, Bardiya (r. 522), ruled only briefly before being assassinated in a palace coup, led by the prince who would become Darius I. His successful suppression of the revolts that followed paved the way for a lengthy reign (r. 522–486), in which he solidified the administrative foundations for an empire that would survive for another century and a half after his death, until the defeat of Darius III (r. 336–330) by Alexander the Great at Issus.

Throughout this period, Judah was an unremarkable, mostly rural outpost, and essentially no Persian records of its history or governance have survived; nor have any contemporaneous native records, outside of the Hebrew Bible. There are, however, administrative and epistolary materials about Jewish life in Persian-period Babylonia and Egypt, from 'Judah-town' (Al-Yahudu) somewhere near Nippur and a military colony at Elephantine, respectively. Herodotus and other Hellenistic historians also offer ample material on the Persians' activities in other areas. Josephus surveys the Persian period from a much later vantage point, in *Antiquities of the Jews* 11.

Isaiah 40–55's distinctive style and historical frame of reference reveal its sixth-century origins. There is a notable change of mood from Isa 40 onward, as the judgement and warnings of looming destruction that dominated the earlier chapters give way to expressions of exultation and confidence. The punishment predicted by Isaiah ben Amoz is now in the past; Judah's 'penalty is paid' (40:2). Second Isaiah also uses distinctive phraseology, vocabulary and imagery, including the figure of the servant and the personification of Zion as a woman, as well as a number of distinctive literary forms and stylistic devices, including hymns, trial speeches and rhetorical questions. Within the Hebrew itself there are also numerous linguistic features that indicate a post-monarchic date. The concerns of Isa 56–66 are generally understood to reflect an even later period, and will be addressed in the next section.

The most obvious reason to recognize Isa 40–55 as stemming from a later period than Isaiah ben Amoz is their explicit reference to people and places dominant in the sixth century. When Isa 45:1 declares, 'Thus says YHWH to his anointed, to Cyrus', this Cyrus is indisputably the sixth-century Persian king. The agent of the people's current situation in exile is identified as the Babylon Empire, whose overwhelming power led to their forebears' defeat and deportation (43:14; 47; 48:14, 20). When Isa 43:14 promises that 'the shouting of the Chaldeans will be turned to lamentation', because YHWH is sending Cyrus 'to perform his purpose on Babylon' (48:14), this message of hope is directed to those whose parents and grandparents were taken from their homeland by a victorious Babylonian army. Such a summons to hope would have been wildly inappropriate – even cruel – if it had been addressed to an eighth-century audience, whose lifetimes would see only judgement, but it is entirely sensible addressed to a sixth-century one.

Among the immediate consequences of the change from Babylonian to Persian imperial rule was an opportunity for those who had been deported by the Babylonians to return to their homelands. Because the exile had lasted more than five decades, in many cases this permission was granted to the children and grandchildren of the original deportees. Not everyone wanted to take advantage of the offer, however; there were still Jewish communities resident in Mesopotamia into the twentieth century CE. Many of the 'exiles' had never seen their ancestral homeland, and understandably preferred to remain in Mesopotamia, where they had been born and put down roots. This is one of the reasons that Second Isaiah was obliged to expend so much energy and space trying to persuade those living in diaspora to 'return' to the homeland (Isa 40).

More subtle indicators of Second Isaiah's sixth-century provenance include its personification of Israel as 'Jacob'. This was much more common after 597 and is especially prominent in Second Isaiah (41:8, 14; 42:24; 43:1, 22, 28; 44:1–2, 5, 21, 22; 45:4, 19; 46:3; 48:1, 12, 20). The stories in Genesis depict Jacob as a migrant who was forced to flee the wrath of his brother and spent much of his life in Mesopotamia, away from his homeland. These traditions are driven by repeated promises of blessing, land and progeny. In broad contours, Jacob's story echoes the experience and aspirations of the Babylonian deportees, who had been driven out of their homeland to Mesopotamia and, at least in the early years, longed to return home. The migrant connection between the community addressed by Second Isaiah and the ancestor Jacob is explicit in Isa 41:8–9, in which Abraham's peripatetic history is also recalled:

> you, Israel, my servant,
>   Jacob, whom I have chosen,
>   the offspring of Abraham, my friend;
> you whom I took from the ends of the earth,
>   and called from its farthest corners,
> saying to you, 'You are my servant,
>   I have chosen you and not cast you off'.

While the whereabouts of Second Isaiah's main audience is clear enough – this material is addressed mainly to the community in Babylonia, which is summoned to undertake a return migration to the ancestors' Levantine homeland – the whereabouts of the prophetic figure(s) who conveyed this message has been a recurring point of contention. Proposals have ranged across the ancient world, from Phoenicia to Egypt and from Babylonia to Judah. Babylonia was the consensus opinion for much of the twentieth century, in part because identifying Second Isaiah with a different geographical setting than the Levantine setting of First Isaiah was seen to support the chronological disjuncture between First and Second Isaiah. More recently, however, the case that Isa 40–55 was composed in the Judahite homeland has been revived by scholars such as Hans Barstad and Lena-Sofia Tiemeyer. Their arguments have sought to rebut a number of older assumptions regarding the poverty of the homeland in the sixth century, as well as placing a greater emphasis on directional markers and agricultural references that suggest a Levantine context (e.g. Cyrus is called 'one from the north' in 41:25).

The problem of the prophet's location can be mitigated (though not fully resolved) by dividing Second Isaiah into Isa 40–48 and 49–55. Isaiah 40–48 exhibits an awareness of Babylonian culture that suggests first-hand encounters with Babylonian deities such as Nabû and Marduk (Nebo and Bel, 46:1), as well as with Babylonian divinatory and astrological sciences (47:9, 12–13). In addition, the core message of these chapters is addressed to the Yahwistic community in Babylonia, calling on them to depart for Jerusalem (48:20). Isaiah 49–55, by contrast, is focused on the restoration of Jerusalem. The prophet and the audience need not necessarily have been in the same place, but the Babylonian focus of Isa 40–48 has tended to be understood as implying a prophet based in Babylonia, where he could speak directly to the exile community; the homeland focus of Isa 49–55, by contrast, has suggested to a greater number of scholars that these chapters could have been written in Jerusalem.

It remains unclear, unfortunately, whether the social and institutional structures of provincial Yehud could have supported the revision of a major prophetic work like the book of Isaiah. Although few now subscribe to some biblical texts' depiction of the land as completely empty (e.g. Jer 42–44), Jerusalem's temple and royal infrastructure had been left in ruins after 586. Whether or to what extent those remaining in the homeland had been able to rebuild and flourish during the intervening decades is frustratingly elusive; the material remains may be interpreted as signs of mere bare-bones survival, or of a reduced but robust social economy.

Barring the discovery of more conclusive extra-biblical evidence, it is impossible to be sure where the prophetic voice behind Second Isaiah's summons to Jerusalem and its vision for the city's restoration was located. It could be the work of a prophet in Babylonia, trying to persuade fellow expatriates to migrate to the land of their ancestors, or it could be the work of a prophet already living in the homeland, who seeks to persuade those in the diaspora to join in efforts to rebuild. That the audience for these exhortations is broader than the Babylonian community is suggested by texts such as Isa 49:12, which invites Jews home from Syene (Aswan); and 45:14–19, which invokes theological terms and ideas associated with the Egyptian god Amun (whose name means 'the Hidden One'). The summons to come to the homeland are addressed to the Egyptian diaspora as well as the Babylonian one.

Arguments regarding the geographical origins of Second Isaiah are thus related to the extent to which these chapters are understood as a unified whole, rather than as a collection of discrete poetic segments. If Isa 40–55 represents the work of a single prophetic voice, a single place of composition is perhaps more likely – although it is also possible that a single prophet made a mid-career move from the diaspora to the homeland, demonstrating his confidence in YHWH's commitment to restoration through his actions as well as his words. If the chapters are a composite work incorporating two or more voices, however, that may explain some of the conflicting evidence for the prophet(s)'s whereabouts.

Despite these lingering uncertainties about geography and composite authorship, it is clear that a significant proportion of the material now comprising the book of Isaiah respond to the political, social and theological circumstances of the late sixth century. As H. G. M. Williamson has argued, these concerns produced not only Isa 40–55, but also several shorter passages earlier in the book, most prominent among them being Isa 2. This chapter provides a sixth-century framework for the older Isaianic traditions, helping a new generation interpret them in a very different context.

Earlier in the sixth century, many of Judah's elites had been deported to Babylonia: a first wave in 597, a second in 586 and probably a third in 582 (2 Kgs 24–25; Jer 52:30). Some of these deportees, including King Jehoiachin and other members of the royal family, were taken to the imperial court in the city of Babylon (2 Kgs 25:27–30). Babylonian documents from this period include lists of the rations allocated to Jehoiachin, his sons and other deportees living at the royal court. Court tales like those of Joseph, Daniel and Esther are mostly from a much later time, but they reflect concerns about integration into the service of foreign empires characteristic of the exilic and post-exilic periods. Extra-biblical evidence also attests to the eventual economic success of some urban members of the deportee community; especially striking are the contracts documenting marriages between descendants of the deportees and native Babylonians.

Other deportees, including the priest Ezekiel, were resettled in more rural areas, where the Babylonians hoped to improve economic productivity by allocating land whose proceeds would later be taxed to feed the imperial coffers. These deportees were faced with a completely different existence than they had had as members of Jerusalem's royal, priestly, and administrative families (2 Kgs 24:12, 14–16). Although this community may have sometimes been obliged to supply workers for imperial building projects, they were not slaves; the arrangement was more like a feudal system, in which the deportees were responsible for the taxable proceeds of the property on which they had been settled. Most of these communities were mono-ethnic; that is, they were dominated by a group of deportees from a single place. One of the effects of this policy was that rural deportees tended to maintain a stronger sense of community and attachment to their homeland; evidence for this may be found in the Yahwistic naming practices of later generations.

In the first years after deportation, most of Jerusalem's former power-brokers were probably focused on survival, learning how to live in a foreign culture, an unfamiliar climate and agricultural environment, and under imperial authority. The books of Jeremiah and Ezekiel testify to early hopes for a rapid return to Jerusalem, dashed by ensuing events (Jer 28; Ezek 13). Thereafter, the deportees may have resigned themselves to settling down and getting on with the necessities, as Jeremiah had advised: 'Build houses and live in them; plant gardens and eat what they produce' (Jer 28:5).

Strikingly, there is almost no record of this period in the surviving biblical texts. Apart from a report of Gedaliah's appointment as provincial governor and subsequent assassination, and a brief note of Jehoiachin's release from Babylonian prison, the books of Kings report nothing of what happened to the land or its people after the defeat of Jerusalem and the destruction of the temple in 586. The book of Lamentations speaks poignantly of the grief occasioned by Jerusalem's fall, perhaps suggesting some form of ongoing liturgy at the site of the ruined temple (cf. Jer 41:5), but appears mainly to describe the immediate aftermath of the disaster, rather than subsequent efforts to find a way forward. The prophetic books of Ezekiel and Jeremiah almost certainly underwent one or more revisions in the exilic period, but their editors chose to reflect on their own circumstances through the lens of the past; they say nothing about the ongoing conditions in Babylonia or Egypt. The biblical texts' reticence regarding this period confirms the extent of the cultural and psychological trauma occasioned by the kingdom's destruction and the uprooting of its inhabitants. If the final chapters of Ezekiel are any indication, hope for restoration survived mainly in the abstract – an idealized vision of the homeland with limited connection to reality (Ezek 40–48).

By the second half of the sixth century, however, the once-invincible Babylonian Empire was on the verge of collapse. Into this context, an anonymous prophet began to speak of a new imperial power, Persia, that would enable the deportees' descendants to return to the ancestral homeland. In Isa 44:28 and 45:1, the leader of this new empire is identified as Cyrus, whose power would eventually extend across the whole of the ancient Near East. Because Second Isaiah's message is so intimately connected to the decline of the Babylonian Empire and the rise of the Persian Empire, it seems most likely that its roots lie in the 540s; Cyrus ascended the Persian throne in 559 and came into the international limelight with his defeat of the Medes in 550. In 539, he conquered Babylon itself, more or less invited into the city by a populace disgruntled with the last Babylonian king, Nabonidus. Second Isaiah is thus usually associated with the decade or so between 550 and 539, as the Babylonian Empire began to crumble and the Persian Empire rose up to succeed it. That at least some of this material predates the fall of Babylon is suggested by the fact that its depictions of the city's demise (e.g. Isa 47) anticipate a degree of destruction that never materialized.

Prior to Babylon's fall, Second Isaiah's proposal that the expatriate community now living in Babylonia ought to uproot itself and move to provincial Jerusalem may have been a tough case to make. Apart from the

Babylonian Empire's apparent invincibility, most of the prophet's audience would have been born in Mesopotamia, not in Judah; the prophet's generation was composed mostly of the children and grandchildren of the original deportees. Few of these people had ever seen the ancestral homeland, only heard stories about it from their parents and grandparents. Data from more recent migrations suggest that a desire to return to and live permanently in the homeland tends to wane in the second and third generations. While the homeland may be symbolically important, and the children and grandchildren of the original migrants may be interested in visiting it, they are not generally inclined to abandon the only lives they have known in favour of 'return' to a homeland in which they have never resided.

This affection for the homeland, but a limited interest in return to it, is especially characteristic of migrants resettled in urban contexts – like the imperial capital of Babylon, whose cosmopolitan atmospheres encourage integration and a pragmatic approach to identity. The city of Babylon plays an important role in Second Isaiah (especially Isa 47), and this may suggest that Second Isaiah's audience included migrants encouraged by their urban, cosmopolitan surroundings to integrate into Babylonian society, even as they maintained some of their own customs. Extra-biblical evidence, especially economic texts dealing with loans and marriages, indicates that at least some deportees and their descendants became financially quite successful, negotiating contracts and commercial deals as part of a thriving imperial economy. There are also marriage contracts between the deportees' offspring and Babylonians – an openness encouraged, perhaps, by Jeremiah's admonition to 'take wives and have sons and daughters; take wives for your sons, and give your daughters in marriage' (Jer 29:6). Persuading these families to abandon the lives they had built in Babylonia to travel to an unfamiliar homeland would not have been easy.

Theological themes and concerns

The sixth-century material in the book of Isaiah is accordingly dominated by persuasive argumentation – sermons, essentially – couched both implicitly and explicitly as a debate with Second Isaiah's detractors. These chapters remind the people living in diaspora that YHWH still cares about them enough to intervene on their behalf, and that YHWH is powerful enough to actually do so. Isaiah 40–48 lay out the argumentative logic behind these declarations; only afterwards can Second Isaiah regale its audience with its vision of a shining Jerusalem at the centre of the nations, overflowing with people worshipping Yʜwʜ on Zion (Isa 49–55). Even then, there are signs that not everyone is fully convinced (49:14).

The major issues of Isa 40–48 appear already in the opening oracle, which serves to summarize the work as a whole:

> See, Yʜwʜ God comes with might,
>   and his arm rules for him;
> his reward is with him,
>   and his recompense before him.
> He will feed his flock like a shepherd;
>   he will gather the lambs in his arms,
> and carry them in his bosom,
>   and gently lead the mother sheep. (40:10–11)

Subsequent chapters lay out the supporting arguments that undergird these bold claims for divine action, affirming Yʜwʜ's ability (and inclination) to rescue a people scattered in diaspora and bring them to their ancestral homeland. These chapters are full of soaring affirmations of Yʜwʜ's power, culminating in a summons to those in the Mesopotamian diaspora to 'go out from Babylon!' (48:20).

These chapters echo a number of the key arguments made by Ezekiel, albeit in much more optimistic terms. The allegation that both prophets seek to deny is that Judah's defeat and the people's subsequent suffering were due to the power of the Babylonians who, assisted by their gods, had overcome Yʜwʜ's efforts to protect his people. Instead, the prophets contend that the kingdom's defeat was a sign of Yʜwʜ's judgement. Thus, the Babylonian king succeeded against Judah not because of the strength of his army, but because Yʜwʜ was using the Babylonians for his own purposes. Although this is a complex theological argument, it sits within a wider ancient Near Eastern tradition in which other gods were said to have abandoned their cities or nations for a time and then returned – including Marduk, the city god of Babylon, in a text called the Marduk Prophecy.

To claim that Yʜwʜ was in control of world events in this way raised significant questions. How could the patron deity of a small, now-defunct kingdom on the imperial margins purport to control the affairs of a military and political machine as powerful as the Babylonian Empire? The prophets' responses draw heavily on traditional Israelite creation theology, even as they adapt it to changed circumstances. Indeed, Second Isaiah makes such extensive use of Israelite creation traditions that this is considered one of Second Isaiah's most significant contributions to the theology of the Hebrew Bible. Specifically, Second Isaiah's depiction of Yhwh as creator of the universe is perhaps the nearest the Hebrew Bible comes to an explicit expression of monotheism: the belief that only one deity exists in the universe. (Monotheism denies other gods' existence, and is distinguished from monolatry, in which adherents worship only one god even if the existence of others is allowed.)

Second Isaiah describes Yhwh's creative acts in soaring language that has made these some of the most beloved of prophetic passages (40:25–31; 45:11–12; 51:12–16, etc.). But these passages are more than just beautiful poetry. When Second Isaiah declares that it is Yhwh 'who created the heavens and stretched them out/who spread out the earth and what comes from it' (42:5; cf. 40:12), this is an assertion of Yhwh's creative authority over creation. The logic is simple but profound: because Yhwh created the universe, Yhwh can act anywhere within it, without opposition.

By extension, to assert that Yhwh is creator of the whole universe, and therefore able to act freely within it, is to claim that Yhwh can act anywhere in the created world *on his people's behalf.* The reason that Second Isaiah so fervently emphasizes Yhwh's universal authority here becomes clear. Yhwh's people are scattered across the world, far from the land in which they once worshipped Yhwh, in an historical moment in which their fate seems entirely subject to foreign imperial powers. In order to persuade this people that Yhwh is able to save them from their exilic circumstances, Second Isaiah needs to establish why and how Yhwh's authority extends beyond Yhwh's traditional homeland in the Levant. (For a vivid example of the perceived territoriality of ancient deities, see 2 Kgs 5.)

Lurking in the background of Second Isaiah's use of creation traditions is an Israelite tradition linking creation, military authority and kingship. The Psalms, in particular, attest to a tradition in which Yhwh's acclamation as the divine King was linked to a demonstration of Yhwh's authority over the forces that threatened creation (e.g. Pss 18; 24; 89; 93). The latter are usually personified as the sea or as one of the large and mysterious creatures that live in the sea, such as Rahab or Leviathan. For example, the psalmist says of Yhwh:

> You rule the raging of the sea;
>> when its waves rise, you still them.
> You crushed Rahab like a carcass;
>> you scattered your enemies with your mighty arm.

The heavens are yours, the earth also is yours;
    the world and all that is in it – you have founded them. …
You have a mighty arm;
    strong is your hand, high your right hand.
Righteousness and justice are the foundation of your throne. (Ps 89:9–11,
13–14)

Anyone who has witnessed a thunderstorm at sea will have an idea of
why the ancients might have viewed the unpredictable and tumultuous
water as dangerous, and used this imagery to depict the threat of universal
disorder that Yhwh's actions stave off. Yhwh's victory against such threats
is memorialized most dramatically in traditions about an epic battle prior to
the creation of the rest of the universe (e.g. Ps 74:12–20). The extant Hebrew
Bible mutes this tradition somewhat, in its efforts to emphasize Yhwh's
status as the sole deity, but it remains the underlying foundation of much of
sixth-century theology.

Second Isaiah's case for Yhwh's global authority, then, depends entirely
on the acclamation of Yhwh as creator: it is only because Yhwh created the
whole of the universe that Yhwh has the authority to bend the Babylonian
and Persian kings to his will. Although Isaiah of Jerusalem had already
alluded to Yhwh's global power and authority (10:5–6), the events of the
sixth century brought the issue even more to the fore. If Yhwh was not in
control of the Babylonian king and his army, if he was only the God of the
land of Judah, then there was no point in worshipping him once the people
were in exile; they were better off throwing their lot in with Marduk, the
patron deity of Babylon.

Second Isaiah accordingly affirms that Judah's defeat and the deportations
to Babylonia occurred at the hands of Yhwh. '*I* profaned the princes of the
sanctuary', Yhwh declares; '*I* delivered Jacob to utter destruction and Israel
to reviling' (43:28). Though such statements strike the modern ear harshly –
accustomed as it is to a near-exclusive emphasis on divine compassion and
affection – Second Isaiah's emphasis on divine responsibility for the people's
misery reiterates that the people's suffering was not the result of some random
confluence of political events, nor the power of the Babylonian king, or his
army, or his gods. The catastrophe was in Yhwh's control, and was permitted
in order to serve Yhwh's own purposes. Although both First and Second
Isaiah acknowledge that foreign empires could go beyond Yhwh's mandate
in their cruelty (e.g. Isa 14; 47), this is not considered a threat to Yhwh's
ultimate control. Second Isaiah focuses instead on the people's suffering

as justifiable judgement for their sins (43:27): this tendency towards self-blame has been usefully explored from the perspective of trauma studies, which suggests that this can be a way of reasserting agency after traumatic disruption.

The practical corollary of Second Isaiah's insistence on YHWH's control over even these most dreadful of events is that YHWH also has the power to reverse the punishment previously inflicted. Therein lies Second Isaiah's twist on the tradition: instead of using a foreign king to punish the people, as had happened in Ezekiel's time, Second Isaiah explains that YHWH will use a foreign king to save them. Just as YHWH acted on a global scale in the past, so YHWH is going to act on a global scale again – but this time it will be for salvation rather than judgement. YHWH has not forgotten the people languishing in Babylonia.

Second Isaiah's argument thus depends on successfully persuading the audience that certain key aspects of YHWH's identity remain intact. If the people believe that YHWH created the universe – not Marduk, as the Babylonians would have it – then they should acknowledge YHWH's authority over the whole of his creation. Moreover, if, as creator, YHWH is still the divine King, then there are two characteristics associated with kingship that remain relevant to their future: YHWH as royal warrior, who will fight for and defend Israel against those wishing to harm it, and YHWH as divine shepherd, who cares for Israel and seeks to promote its well-being.

Almost the entirety of Isaiah 40–48 is devoted to these aspects of YHWH's identity. The affirmation that YHWH is king is foremost: because a claim to kingship is tantamount to a claim to power, nothing can proceed until YHWH's kingship is firmly established. Royal imagery pervades Second Isaiah, and YHWH's divine kingship is explicitly asserted in Isa 41:21; 43:15; 44:6; and 52:7 ('your God reigns'). The particular emphasis varies – sometimes the continuity of YHWH's claim to kingship is the focus, and sometimes the pre-eminence of YHWH's royal status over other aspects of the divine character is foregrounded. But perhaps the most noteworthy aspect of this royal rhetoric is Second Isaiah's emphasis on the exclusivity of YHWH's claim to be king – YHWH alone is king, and no other.

In the opening oracle, for example, a herald announces YHWH's impending arrival (40:3–4) with reference to his royal majesty (40:5). YHWH's kingship is linked to dominance over the nations (40:10, 15–17, 28), as well as his role as a benevolent shepherd who cares for his people like a flock of sheep (40:11, 14, 29–31). YHWH's claim to these royal roles is founded on his creative works: who but YHWH 'has measured the waters in the hollow of his hand, and marked off the heavens with a span' (40:12, 28)? As the preponderance of rhetorical questions highlights (40:12–14, 18–19, 21, 25–26), one of the central issues in Second Isaiah concerns Yhwh's incomparability: 'Who is my equal?' (40:25). 'Who is like me?' (44:7). Second Isaiah's contention is that no other gods have the knowledge Yhwh has, no other gods have the power Yhwh has over creation, and no other gods have done what Yhwh has done: 'I am the first and I am the last; besides me there is no god' (44:6). It is Yhwh and no other who sits enthroned as king above the earth (40:22). These assertions are crucial evidence in Second Isaiah's argument that Yhwh is going act on behalf of the people languishing in diaspora. As superlative and incomparable, Yhwh's authority is unchallenged. He is *able* to save Israel – and thus there is reason to think that he will do so.

As part of these efforts to establish Yhwh's superlative status, Second Isaiah spends significant time denigrating other deities. One of the forms this takes is the so-called idol polemic, in which the prophet hurls abuse at the physical objects representing the presence of other deities, and at the people who worship them. This strategy surfaces early, in the opening chapter, which demands to know if Second Isaiah's audience would be so bold as to compare Yhwh to one of these objects: 'to whom then will you liken God, or what likeness compare with him? An idol?' (40:18–19).

This and other polemical passages foreground the materiality of these objects, depicting them as lifeless pieces of wood: the artisan who creates them uses one piece to fuel his dinner fire, another to create an object he worships as a god (44:9–20). The resulting objects may be beautiful, made of rare woods and adorned with precious metals, but they are lifeless as stone (40:19–20; 44:12–14). Second Isaiah goes on to mock those who expect these gods to save them, when they cannot even move about on their own – their worshippers have to carry the statues about for them (45:20). The picture of idols loaded onto animals in order to be transported into captivity, after they have failed to protect their worshippers, is particularly absurd (46:1–2).

Second Isaiah's rhetoric regarding these objects is almost certainly a satire of actual ancient beliefs about divine statues. Foreign gods were not thought to be stuck in their statues; rather, the statues served to provide a space, or a conduit, for the deities' earthly presence to be accessible to their worshippers. After the physical object was made, a statue was inducted into cultic use in an elaborate pair of rites, the 'opening of the mouth' and 'the washing of the mouth', which sanctified the statues and prepared them for the divine presence. These rites were intended to effect an existential transformation of the object, so that it was not only what it appeared to be – a highly adorned, human-made object – but also something more. (Conceptually, this is not far distant from the belief in the transformation of ordinary bread and wine into the body and blood of Christ, in Christian communities that hold to the doctrine of transubstantiation.)

There was accordingly a sense in which these cult statues were understood to be very closely connected to the gods they represented and to their powers – hence it was possible for a conquering power to 'godnap' a deity, capturing a god's statue and 'deporting' it to the capital of the conquering power. This phenomenon is perhaps what lies behind Isa 46, in which Second Isaiah scoffs at worshippers taking care to load up the statues of Bel (Marduk) and Nebo (Nabû) onto the donkeys accompanying them into exile.

For much of the twentieth century these idol polemics were isolated from the rest of Second Isaiah's argument, supposing that they had originally circulated separately and only belatedly been inserted into Second Isaiah. While it remains possible to argue that these passages are secondary – some, including the longest such passage in Isa 44:9–20, are more prose-like than the rest of Second Isaiah – it has been increasingly appreciated that they have an important function in their current contexts, namely, to contrast the foreign gods and their 'lifeless' statues with YHWH, to the point of making the worship of those gods seem absurd and pointless. Thus, these passages always appear in the context of Second Isaiah's arguments about YHWH's power and authority (Isa 40–48). If these passages did originate separately, they now comprise a critical pillar of Second Isaiah's case.

These denials of other deities' powers are frequently intertwined with Second Isaiah's assertions of YHWH's own power. One of the key arguments in this regard concerns YHWH's knowledge: one proof of YHWH's authority over the universe and its workings is that YHWH has unsurpassed knowledge of past, present and future events. 'Who has announced from of old the things to come?', Second Isaiah asks. 'Let them tell us what is yet to be! Do not fear, or be afraid; have I not told you from of old and declared it? You are my witnesses!', says YHWH (44:7). Rhetorical questions of this sort are typical of Second Isaiah; speaking as if to a jury, Second Isaiah summons potential witnesses to present evidence. Failure to appear is a sign of the weakness of the opposition's case. YHWH, by contrast, dominates the witness stand. His ready knowledge of both past and future reflects his sole control over world history – a control that is essential to his ability to act on Israel's behalf in future (41:21–24; 42:9; 43:9-10; 46:8–11; 48:3–5).

This divine knowledge is conveyed to the people through Yʜwʜ's prophets. The prophets communicate divine warnings about coming events and, in the process, witness to Yʜwʜ's foreknowledge about those events. Because Yʜwʜ created the universe and has control over all that occurs within it, Yʜwʜ knows what has been, what is and what will be. Yʜwʜ's prophets thus function as critical witnesses to Yʜwʜ's authority, and Second Isaiah explicitly connects assertions of Yʜwʜ's creative powers with declarations of Yʜwʜ's knowledge conveyed through his chosen representatives. Thus:

I am Yʜwʜ who made all things,
>who alone stretched out the heavens,
>who by myself spread out the earth;
who frustrates the omens of liars,
>and makes fools of diviners;
who turns back the wise,
>and makes their knowledge foolish;
who confirms the word of his servant,
>and fulfils the prediction of his messengers. (44:24–26)

As creator, Yʜwʜ stands in full control of all creation, knowing all that happens within it and demonstrating that knowledge via Yʜwʜ's servants the prophets. No other nations and no other gods can claim such knowledge (43:10; 48:5).

These passages also reveal an important element of Second Isaiah's argument in favour of Yʜwʜ's sole divine authority – namely, that if other deities do exist, they have proven themselves to be so ineffective that they might as well not exist. At the very least, they do not merit the appellation of 'god'. Thus, Yʜwʜ goes from the observation that 'besides me there is no saviour' (43:11) to the conclusion that 'besides me there is no god' (44:6; 45:5; cf. 44:8; 45:6, 14, 21). This is one of the Hebrew Bible's most explicit declarations of monotheism.

As the only effective deity left standing, Yʜwʜ's authority over history is unchallenged. Although worked out in much greater detail over the course of Isa 40–48, Second Isaiah's claims in this regard are prominent from the beginning: it is Yʜwʜ

who sits above the circle of the earth,
>and its inhabitants are like grasshoppers;
who stretches out the heavens like a curtain,
>and spreads them like a tent to live in;
who brings princes to naught,
>and makes the rulers of the earth as nothing. (40:22–23)

As creator of the universe and lord of history, YHWH has both the authority and the capacity to bring about radical change in the exiles' circumstances. Even the mighty empires, declares Second Isaiah, are subject to YHWH's will.

In an earlier era, YHWH would have achieved his plans for corporate salvation through the king in Jerusalem. But there is no such king, so YHWH must act via other means. After several chapters of build-up, and with a final reminder of his own creative authority, YHWH announces that he now plans to work through the Persian king, Cyrus: 'He is my shepherd, and he shall carry out all my purpose' (44:28). Even more shockingly, this is followed by a description of Cyrus as YHWH's anointed (*mashiach*; 45:1), using terminology associated with the Davidic king in order to identify him as the means by which YHWH will exert his authority over the foreign nations and enable his people to return to their homeland:

> Thus says YHWH to his anointed, to Cyrus,
>   whose right hand I have grasped
> to subdue nations before him
>   and strip kings of their robes,
> to open doors before him –
>   and the gates shall not be closed:
> I will go before you
>   and level the mountains,
> I will break in pieces the doors of bronze
>   and cut through the bars of iron,
> I will give you the treasures of darkness
>   and riches hidden in secret places,
> so that you may know that it is I, YHWH,
>   the God of Israel, who call you by your name.
> For the sake of my servant Jacob,
>   and Israel my chosen,
> I call you by your name,
>   I surname you, though you do not know me.
> I am YHWH, and there is no other;
>   besides me there is no god.
> I arm you, though you do not know me,
> so that they may know, from the rising of the sun
>   and from the west, that there is no one besides me;
>   I am YHWH, and there is no other. (45:1–6)

It is difficult to overstate how startling this declaration would have been to its original audience. Foreign kings were normally used punitively, as Nebuchadnezzar had been, not as the means of Israel's salvation.

Deuteronomy 17:15 expressly forbids such a thing: 'You are not permitted to put a foreigner over you, who is not of your own community.'

The unexpected nature of YHWH's plan is one reason that the preceding arguments for YHWH's authority are so lengthy; the prophet had to be absolutely sure that the people were convinced of YHWH's abilities before springing upon them such an unexpected deployment of them. Assertions of YHWH's royal authority – and of his intentions to use that authority on Israel's behalf – thus become increasingly explicit and increasingly insistent as the announcement of Cyrus as YHWH's agent approaches. YHWH is repeatedly identified as Israel's king (44:6; cf. Isa 41:21; 43:15), saviour (43:3, 11, 12; 45:15, 17, 21, 22) and redeemer (41:14; 43:1, 14; 44:6, 22–24). YHWH's actions may appear unconventional, but they are the actions of Israel's God and are undertaken for Israel's salvation.

Indeed, as the announcement of Cyrus draws near, reminders of YHWH's creative activities focus increasingly on Israel, with sweeping affirmations of YHWH as creator of heaven and earth reinforced by more specific references to YHWH as Creator of Israel (43:1, 7, 15; 44:2, 21, 24). Alongside these declarations are a number of possible allusions to the exodus and wilderness traditions, including the crossing of the Sea of Reeds (43:1–2, 16–17; 44:27; cf. 50:2; 51:10; 52:11–12), the way through the wilderness (43:19–21; cf. 40:3; 48:21) and YHWH's bringing of the people to the homeland (43:4–7). Second Isaiah purposely blurs the distinction between the exodus as a past event, which proves YHWH's earthly power and interventionist care for Israel, and the exodus as a model for, or a way of talking about, Israel's future restoration – a 'second exodus'.

These references to Israel's past history with YHWH effect a gradual narrowing of the focus of earthly activities of YHWH. Second Isaiah begins broadly, emphasizing YHWH's universal authority as king and creator of heavens and earth and victor over the nations (Isa 41–42), then moves towards a more specific emphasis on YHWH as king and creator of Israel and victor over Egypt on Israel's behalf (Isa 43–44). This should not be construed as a narrowing of Second Isaiah's claim's regarding YHWH's power; rather, it constitutes a narrowing of Second Isaiah's rhetorical attention, using a case study familiar and compelling to the audience in order to remind and persuade the people of YHWH's global power: YHWH's actions with regard to Israel are historically specific manifestations of YHWH's universal control as creator of the universe.

The intimate connection between YHWH as king and creator of the universe and YHWH as king and creator of Israel is reiterated in the final run-up to the naming of Cyrus (44:28); the announcement itself is immediately followed by a lengthy reiteration of YHWH's global authority as creator (45:7–19). The overall effect is to convey the claim that, in the same way YHWH exerted his royal power in the past – over the whole created order at creation, then later on Israel's particular behalf, especially in the exodus – now YHWH is exerting his royal power through Cyrus (cf. 48:14–15, 20–21).

The announcement of Cyrus is then followed by one more derisive summons to the nations: come forth and prove the abilities of their gods (45:20–21). The silence is a sign that YHWH's claim to be the power behind Cyrus is refutable. The point is elaborated again and at greater length in Isa 46, in which the prophet mocks the helplessness of rival deities in another iteration of the idol polemic. Stripped of these deities' protection, Babylon's downfall is assured (Isa 47). The argument climaxes with a resounding recapitulation of YHWH's creative powers, witnessed by his foreknowledge and manifest in his will to act (Isa 48).

Given the radically new emphasis of much of this material – especially its positivity, in the wake of false prophets preaching 'peace' when there was none (Jer 6:14; 8:11; 14:13; 28:5–11; Ezek 13:9–16) – it is not surprising that the prophet(s) behind Second Isaiah sought to establish the credibility of these claims by relying heavily on the language, style and even actual prophecies of earlier prophets, and thus emphasizing the continuity of this new prophetic message with that which had come before.

Second Isaiah has especially close connections with the earlier Isaianic material; it also exhibits extensive links to Jeremiah, as well as to other prophetic and non-prophetic texts. Sometimes Second Isaiah affirms an earlier oracle: Isa 42:18–25 refers to 30:9–14; Isa 40:2 uses Jer 16:18; and Isa 41:25 and 64:8 reprise the metaphor of the Lord as potter (Isa 29:15; cf. Jer 18). Often, however, these chapters take older material and reinterpret it. The opening poem of Isa 40:1–10, for example, uses words of judgement from Isa 28:1–5 in order to proclaim a message of hope and restoration; the joyful proclamation of coming restoration in Isa 54:1–5 reverses the judgement of Jer 10:17–25; and much of the description of Jerusalem's coming restoration inverts the depiction of the bereaved city in the Book of Lamentations (e.g. Isa 40:1 and Lam 1:2; Isa 51:19–20 and Lam 2:19; and Isa 54:4 and Lam 1:1). Second Isaiah also makes use more broadly of theological ideas and language already familiar from older texts, such as Isaiah ben Amoz's emphasis on YHWH as the 'Holy One of Israel' (a title also used in certain psalms) and Deuteronomy's use of the name Jeshurun for Israel (Deut 32:15; 33:5, 26; Isa 44:2) and its depiction of YHWH as Israel's Rock (Deut 32; Isa 44:8; 51:1).

One of the most common rhetorical forms in Second Isaiah is the oracle of salvation. Like much of Second Isaiah's language and style, this tradition is likely to have had its roots in the Jerusalem temple, conveying Yhwh's words of assurance to a worshipper who had come to lament his or her current plight. (The most direct proof of the existence of oracles of salvation occurring as response to laments is Lam 3:55–57 and Ps 35:1–3). Second Isaiah uses the oracle of salvation to respond to the lamentations of the people living in diaspora: using in a form familiar from the liturgy, Second Isaiah reassures them that Yhwh does still hear their laments, and will respond to them with saving power. Isaiah 44:1–5 is a good example: it summons the people to listen – 'Hear, O Jacob my servant!' (44:1) – then assures them that they have nothing to fear from their current circumstances (44:2), because Yhwh will intervene on their behalf (44:3). The people will flourish (44:4), and recognize Yhwh's authority (44:5).

It is possible that parts of Second Isaiah could have been initially delivered in a liturgical setting; although very little is known of the deportees' religious practices in Mesopotamia, it is generally assumed that they must have gathered together for worship in some form (the challenges of this are noted most poignantly by Psalm 137). It has been argued, for example, that Second Isaiah represents a cultic drama, or that the anonymous prophet might have been a liturgical singer. It has generally been assumed that the deity's response to a petitioner's supplication would have been conveyed by a priest, but the line between priests and prophets is a somewhat fluid one (compare, for example, the priest-prophet Ezekiel, and Isaiah of Jerusalem's apparent familiarity with the inner parts of the Jerusalem temple). The extent of the liturgy-like material in Second Isaiah perhaps suggests another prophetic figure(s) familiar with the temple and its liturgical traditions.

There are also a number of hymns of praise in these chapters. This, too, is a liturgical genre; the psalter suggests that such hymns were used in the Jerusalem temple. It seems likely that similar hymns would have been used by worshipping communities in diaspora, as well. The hymns summon the people to praise Yhwh, reminding them of the wonderful things Yhwh has done to merit their praise. Psalm 117 is a short but neat example:

'Praise Yhwh, all you nations!
　Extol him, all you peoples!
For great is his steadfast love towards us,
　and the faithfulness of Yhwh endures forever.
Praise Yhwh!'

Isaiah 49:13 comes just as quickly to the point, with the twist that it is the whole of YHWH's creation that is summoned to praise YHWH for his actions on the people's behalf: 'Sing for joy, O heavens, and exult, O earth; break forth, O mountains, into singing! For YHWH has comforted his people, and will have compassion on his suffering ones.' Hymnic participles in the Hebrew emphasize that YHWH's benevolence and care for the people are ongoing; although often translated in the past tense, they are often signalled in English with 'who' phrases (e.g. 44:24–28). A clearer translation might read:

> Thus says YHWH, your Redeemer –
>   the one who forms you in the womb –
> I am YHWH, who makes all things,
>   who alone stretches out the heavens,
>   who by myself spreads out the earth … (44:24)

Second Isaiah uses these traditions to press its audience to recognize the implications of the words they are reciting in their communal worship contexts. In their liturgy, they say that they believe that YHWH is the Creator of heaven and earth; if they truly believe those words, then they should believe that YHWH can act to save them (40:18–26). Indeed, why would they ever doubt YHWH's power to intervene on their behalf, by whatever means necessary (45:9–13)? The emphatic function of the hymns is apparent from the fact that they often come at the end of major sections, marking key stages in Second Isaiah's argument. For example, the first half of Second Isaiah culminates with an exhortation:

> Go out from Babylon, flee from Chaldea,
>   declare this with a shout of joy, proclaim it,
> send it forth to the end of the earth;
>   say, 'YHWH has redeemed his servant Jacob!' (48:20)

The second half of Second Isaiah (Isa 49–55) turns to the glorious future in Jerusalem that awaits those who heed this call and return to Jerusalem. These chapters prioritize the image of YHWH as Redeemer (49:7, 26; 50:2; 51:10; 52:3, 9; 54:5, 8; cf. Isa 47:4; 48:17, 20) and use both male and female metaphorical language to describe the effects and purposes of YHWH's redeeming actions.

One of the most striking aspects of Second Isaiah's depiction of Jerusalem's restoration is its extensive, multifaceted use of overtly feminine imagery – wife, mother, daughter – for the city and its inhabitants (49:14–21; 50:1–3; 51:17–21; 52:1–6; 54:1–10; cf. 62:1–5; 66:7–13). Second Isaiah exploits this personification of the city to make a series of points regarding YHWH's power to transform it and its inhabitants. These metaphors were embedded in the languages of the ancient Semitic world, in which cities were linguistically feminine. They also presume that the audience had certain cultural ideas about women and their social roles.

For example, Second Isaiah's Jerusalem-as-wife-and-mother metaphor has roots in the so-called prophetic marriage metaphor. In Hosea, Jeremiah and Ezekiel, the fidelity expected of a woman in ancient Israel to her husband is used as a metaphor through which to describe the fidelity due to YHWH by YHWH's people, Israel. At its best, this material evokes the deep pain of a betrayed spouse to articulate the grief and the fury of God betrayed by Israel. But the prophets' use of marriage as a metaphor for this relationship presupposes an unequal distribution of power between the two parties to the marriage; while this appears to have been typical in the ancient world, and in the modern one until quite recently, the disconnect between ancient and modern conceptualizations of the relationship between husband and wife means that these passages can be troublesome for contemporary readers. The rhetorical extremes to which the text goes to describe God's anger are hazardous if taken as licence for such behaviour on the part of humans, as scholars such as Katheryn Pfisterer Darr and Julie M. O'Brien have emphasized.

Though the metaphor may be traced at least to Hosea, it is especially prominent in the sixth-century prophetic literature of Jeremiah and Ezekiel. There, the destruction of Jerusalem by YHWH and the deportation of its inhabitants to Babylonia are likened to the wrath of a betrayed husband and his decision to divorce an unfaithful wife (Jer 3:1–18; Ezek 16; 23). The violence of YHWH's treatment of Israel in these texts derives in part from the fact that Israel's abandonment of YHWH is understood as provoking YHWH's reciprocal abandonment of Israel. Descriptions of Israel's punishment for infidelity therefore blur into more general depictions of the consequences of YHWH's withdrawal of divine protection: the Israelites will be humiliated by their enemies and the natural world will no longer provide for them.

The metaphorical imagining of the original deportees from Jerusalem as divorcées forms the background for YHWH's questions to the current generation in Second Isaiah: 'Where is your mother's bill of divorce, with which I sent her away?' (50:1). The oracle goes on to declare that, while both the previous generation and this one were exiled because of their sins, YHWH retains the power now to call them back to inhabit the city they were forced to abandon. Speaking to Jerusalem, YHWH admits that 'for a brief moment, I deserted you', but now offers a solemn oath 'that I will not be angry with you, and will not rebuke you … my steadfast love shall not depart from you, and my covenant of peace shall not be removed' (54:9–10). The promise is akin to that offered to Noah: never again (54:9; cf. Gen 9:11). If taken as a model for human marital relationships, Yhwh's vacillation between punitive wrath and expressions of favour is dangerously akin to the destructive patterns of an abusive spouse. If the distinction between what is possible for humans and what is possible for God is clearly maintained, Yhwh's intervention in Jerusalem's grief, transforming it into shouts of joy and delight, may be more positively construed; Yhwh sees Jerusalem's distress and acts to ameliorate it. Lamentation is transformed into joy. Given the family frame of the metaphor, it may also be relevant to consider whether such promises were intended only for the current generation, whom Yhwh deems to have been punished enough, or are made in perpetuity, regardless of the behaviour of future children.

As in earlier prophetic material (e.g., Ezek 16:4–7), Second Isaiah's personification of Jerusalem blurs together images of the city as a wife and images of the city as a daughter. This latter aspect of the city's metaphorical presence is signalled most explicitly through the city's description as 'Daughter Zion', who is summoned to 'Awake!' and 'Rise up!' in response to the good news that her people are about to return (52:1–2; cf. 62:11). Although Isa 52 is the only time that the title appears explicitly in Isa 40–55, the unnamed female interlocutor of much of Second Isaiah's latter half is rightly understood to be this 'Daughter Zion' (49:14–21; 50:1–3; 51:17–21; 52:1–6; 54:1–10, cf. 62:1–5; 66:7–13).

For such an important figure, it is unfortunate that the exact significance of the title 'Daughter (of) Zion' (*bat Zion*) remains unclear. Other biblical texts suggest that to speak of a woman as 'daughter of [place]' is to signal that the woman is (or was formerly) resident in that particular city. If this is the main point, then the 'Daughter of Zion' language imagines an unnamed female resident of Jerusalem (Zion), whose experience is used by the prophetic literature to speak about the experiences of the inhabitants of the city as a whole (compare 'daughter Judah' in Lam 2:2, 5; 'daughter Egypt' in Jer 46:19, 24; 'daughter Dibon' in Jer 48:18; and Ps 45:12 [ET], where NRSV translates an analogous phrase as 'the people of Tyre').

But the title 'daughter Zion' also functions to personify the city itself. Second Isaiah's use in this sense draws especially on the book of Lamentations, which it seems to know in written form. Lamentations shares a number of features with an ancient Near Eastern literary genre known as the city laments, in which a city's patron goddess laments its destruction. This goddess is imagined as a maternal figure, with the city's inhabitants identified as her children; the city's patron (parental) deity therefore bears a special responsibility for the people's protection and well-being. These wider cultural conventions may explain why Second Isaiah uses the title 'Daughter Zion' specifically in the context of a passage emphasizing Jerusalem's formerly sorry state, in contrast to the glorious restoration now anticipated (52:2, cf. 62:11).

Given the nature of poetic and metaphorical language, it is likely that both the city and its inhabitants are in view in these passages. To an ancient audience, the daughter language would have placed a special emphasis not only on the value of the city, but also on its inhabitants' vulnerability to physical danger and external threats: the emotional associations of femininity in the ancient Near East revolved especially around women's and children's vulnerability in contexts of military and sexualized violence. Similar associations are evident in the passage about Daughter Babylon in Isa 47, in which widowhood and loss of children are especially prominent (47:3, 8–9).

Recognizing that the book of Lamentations stands prominently in the background of these chapters is crucial for making sense of what they are trying to do, as well as how they are trying to do it. A connection with Lamentations is already apparent from Second Isaiah's first description of the city (49:8–50:3). There, Zion speaks for the only time in Second Isaiah. Though brief, her words encapsulate the crux of the accusation against which Second Isaiah seeks to defend YHWH: 'YHWH has forsaken me', Zion declares; 'my lord has forgotten me!' (49:14). The words placed in Zion's mouth are almost a direct quotation of Lam 5:20, where they appear in the final, exhausted conclusion to Lamentations, as five chapters of acute distress end with a question and a plea:

> Why have you forgotten us completely?
>   Why have you forsaken us these many days?
> Restore us to yourself, YHWH, that we may be restored;
>   renew our days as of old –
> unless you have utterly rejected us,
>   and are angry with us beyond measure. (Lam 5:20–22)

In Lamentations, these questions go unanswered; YHWH, who has been silent throughout, makes no last-minute appearance to deny that he has abandoned the city and its people, or that the divine wrath is anything but absolute.

This and other connections between Lamentations and Second Isaiah suggest that one of Second Isaiah's aims in using the Daughter Zion image is to offer a deliberate, almost point-by-point response to concerns raised by previous generations but never adequately answered. The apparent lack of divine response to the city's lamentation, in particular, is addressed by Second Isaiah with gusto: here Yhwh barely ceases talking, chapter after chapter.

Second Isaiah is dedicated, in particular, to rebutting any lingering claim that Yhwh has abandoned Jerusalem: Lamentations' repeated claim – that Jerusalem 'has no one to comfort her' (Lam 1:2, 9, 17, 21; cf. 1:16; 2:13) – is not (or is no longer) true. 'I' – declares Yhwh, 'I am he, your comforter!' (Isa 51:12). Likewise, 'Yhwh has comforted Zion; he has comforted all her waste places' (51:3). Second Isaiah's opening imperative – 'Comfort, O comfort my people' (40:1) anticipated this theme; in its latter half, it is unpacked at length.

The loss and anticipated restoration of Zion's children (the city's inhabitants) are also prominent in these two texts, exploiting the metaphor of Jerusalem as a woman to transform the city who has been abandoned by her (divine) husband and bereft of her children (inhabitants) into a wife blessed with numerous children. Lamentation begins with an observation of the city's desolation – 'How lonely sits the city that was full of people!' (Lam 1:1) – and returns to the theme several times (1:16, 18; 2:11–12, 19–22; 4:2–8). Second Isaiah quotes these texts, as it prepares to assure the city of its inhabitants' return (e.g. Isa 51:20 cf. Lam 2:11; 4:1; Isa 51:22 cf. Lam 4:11, 21). The children's restoration – the repopulation of the city – is addressed first in Isa 49:14–26, in which Zion hears that the children whom she had lost will now be so numerous in her streets that they will complain there is no room (49:20, cf. 54:1–3). Her inhabitants will be like the adornments of a bride (49:18).

Whether Second Isaiah succeeds in persuading Daughter Zion of Yhwh's words of comfort is unclear: Second Isaiah never describes the city's response to Yhwh's assertions. Perhaps Jerusalem, like a wife whose husband has made such promises before (54:9), is yet to be convinced that real change is coming. When Zion says that 'Yhwh has forsaken me, indeed my Lord has forgotten me' (49:14), Yhwh's attempt to reassure her – 'Can a woman forget her nursing child, that she should have no compassion on the son of her womb?' (49:15) – recalls the agonized question of Lamentations: 'Should women eat their offspring, their infant children?' (Lam 2:20). Inadvertently or otherwise, Yhwh's claim that divine love surpasses even that of a mother for her child invokes a reminder that, in a post-586 world, even the most steadfast of commitments can be cast into doubt.

Insofar as Daughter Zion represents the city of Jerusalem and its inhabitants, it may be that she has cause to doubt. One of the most striking aspects of Second Isaiah's use – and frequent inversion – of material from Lamentations is that these chapters take concerns originally raised by the surviving inhabitants of Jerusalem – that is, those left in the homeland – and addresses them to those who had been deported. Although the distinction between 'those left behind' and 'those taken into exile' is likely to have been blurred by repeated deportations – those 'left behind' after 597 may have been taken into exile in 586 or 582 – Second Isaiah's emphasis on the necessity of returning to Jerusalem is nevertheless pronounced. Uncertainty in the homeland as to whether this is 'good news' for those who have survived in the city would turn out to be justified; as attested in Ezra–Nehemiah, especially, many of those who would arrive in Jerusalem from Babylonia viewed themselves as superior to those whom they found in the city.

In addition to Lamentations Second Isaiah is also in dialogue with a number of other biblical texts, including earlier parts of the book of Isaiah, prophetic material from the book of Jeremiah, and especially the psalms. The prediction of destruction that culminates Isaiah of Jerusalem's call vision in Yʜᴡʜ's throne room (6:11–13), for instance, is echoed in a number of Second Isaiah's promises of restoration (49:8, 19; 51:3; 52:9; 54:3; cf. 61:4). Like the first half of Second Isaiah, these allusions to other biblical traditions work to assert the basic continuity of its message with the older traditions, even as it frequently turns them on their heads.

As scholars such as Patricia Tull Willey have charted, sometimes this re-use of older materials can be quite complex. So, for example, Isa 52:7–11 draws on three distinct older texts (Nah 1:15 [Hebrew 2:1]; Ps 98:3; Lam 4:15), as it re-imagines their significance in Second Isaiah's new, sixth-century context. The allusions are somewhat difficult to recognize in the NRSV, so modified versions of these passages are presented here to make the connections clearer.

'How beautiful upon the mountains are the feet of a messenger, the one who announces peace, messenger of good news, who announces salvation.' (Isa 52:7)	'Look! On the mountains are the feet of a messenger, one who announces peace!' (Nah 1:15).

In this case, Second Isaiah takes the Nahum text, repeats a significant portion of it, and then expands the oracle through repetition of the key terms 'messenger' (*mebasser*) and 'one who announces' (*mashmia'*). Then, a few verses later, it does a similar thing with Ps 98, taking key terms from three successive verses in the psalm to formulate a re-statement of YHWH's global power:

'YHWH has bared his holy arm in the sight of all the nations, and all the ends of the earth will see the salvation of our God' (Isa 51:10)	'… his holy arm … ' (Ps 98:1) '… in the sight of the nations … ' (Ps 98:2) '… all the ends of the earth will see the salvation of our God' (Ps 98:3)

As the selection of phrases suggests, Second Isaiah's use of the psalms is related to its interest in YHWH's power, authority, and ability to act on the people's behalf worldwide. That Ps 98 – alluded to also in Isa 42:10–12; 44:23; 49:13; 51:3; 52:10; 55:12 – is one of Second Isaiah's favourite source texts is not surprising; it is one of the psalms that most vociferously declares that YHWH is king and reigns over all the earth.

Finally, Second Isaiah takes a passage from Lamentations:

'"Depart! Depart! Go out from there! Do not touch anything unclean; go out from its midst, purify yourselves, you who carry the vessels of YHWH!"' (Isa 52:11)	'"Depart! Unclean!" they cried at them; "Depart! Depart! Do not touch!" So they fled and wandered; they said among the nations, "They will continue to migrate."' (Lam 4:15)

As with much of Second Isaiah's use of Lamentations, the text draws on the older material to signal the people's reversal of fortune: the people who had been defiled by the city's destruction have been purified through exile and must take care not to touch the unclean things of the nations as they depart. The watchmen who scanned the horizon hopelessly in search of human salvation (Lam 4:17) will be the first to see signs of YHWH's return to Zion (Isa 52:8). The roads to Zion that were full of mourning (Lam 1:4) will be full of jubilant song (Isa 51:11). The city bereft of its children (Lam 1:1, 16, 18; 2:11–12, 19–22; 4:2–8) will be repopulated beyond measure (Isa 49:20, cf. 54:1–3). The city without comfort will be comforted.

At several points, Second Isaiah describes individuals and groups as YHWH's 'servant' (*'ebed*). In the early twentieth century, scholars isolated four of these passages from their surroundings and argued that they had originally circulated as independent 'Servant Songs' (42:1–4[9]; 49:1–6; 50:4–9[11]; 52:13–53:12). The identity of the 'servant' in these passages subsequently became a topic of significant dispute. Some argued that the servant was a single individual: the prophet, an anonymous teacher of the law, an idealized individual like Moses, or even Cyrus. In arguments in favour of the servant as the prophet, for example, Isa 42:1–4 is identified as a prophetic call scene, in which the prophet is commissioned by YHWH (the first-person speaker) to 'bring forth justice to the nations'.

Others have argued that the 'servant' is not a single individual but rather a representative of a larger group, which is usually identified as the entire Israelite community in Babylonia. This identification of YHWH's servant with Israel is explicit the first time that the term ʿebed appears in Second Isaiah: 'You, Israel, my servant, Jacob, whom I have chosen … do not fear, for I am with you' (41:8, 10). The same identification and same reassurance appear again a few chapters later: 'hear, O Jacob my servant, Israel whom I have chosen! … Do not fear, O Jacob my servant, Jeshurun whom I have chosen' (44:1–2). YHWH's redeeming activities on Israel's behalf are also the focus of other passages that identify Israel as YHWH's servant (44:21; 45:4; 48:20). The events of the servant's 'career' – including his call and special status, suffering and subsequent restoration – are here seen in terms of Israel's own history, as depicted in Second Isaiah: election (41:8; 51:2), current suffering (40:2), and coming restoration (throughout). This use of ʿebed for Israel appears exclusively in the first half of Second Isaiah, in the chapters most focused on persuading the people of YHWH's determination to act on their behalf.

The depiction of the servant suffering innocently, however, is not in keeping with the way that Israel is otherwise characterized in Second Isaiah (53:7–8). Despite its acute distress at the people's situation, none of the prophetic literature of this period claims that Israel suffers in innocence; rather it emphasizes Israel's sinful behaviour as the just cause of its punishment. Other stumbling blocks to an interpretation of the servant as Israel include the servant's depiction as having a mission *to* Israel (49:5) and the fact that an anonymous first-person plural voice ('we') speaks *about* the servant in the final servant song (53:2–6): if this plural speaking body is not Israel, its identity is quite mysterious.

One of the difficulties in attempts to identify the servant is the rarity of the imagery used in the last servant song (52:13–53:12). There, the servant may be depicted as suffering vicariously on behalf of a wider, sinful community. Vicarious suffering, especially of an individual, is quite unusual within the Hebrew Bible; this means that there are limited other texts that might be used to inform an interpretation of this passage. The Isaiah text is also open to multiple readings, because there is significant variation among the ancient witnesses (this is reflected in the variety of translations offered by commentators and Bible translators). The Aramaic translation in Targum Jonathan, for example, reads the instruction to 'Behold my servant' in Isa 52:13 as 'Behold my servant, the Messiah'. This messianic interpretation of the servant is also taken up in some early rabbinic texts, which connect the description of the servant who suffers to the messiah who will intercede with God on Israel's behalf (b. Sanh. 98b; Rab. Ruth 5:6; compare also Pesiq. Rab. 36:4). Later Jewish interpretation, including major medieval rabbinic commentators such as Rashi, has tended instead to view the servant as representative of the community as a whole, whose suffering is prelude to eventual restoration.

The interpretation of the servant imagery in general, and Isa 53 in particular, has been further complicated by the heavy weight of Christian interpretive tradition, which has viewed the latter as a description of Jesus's suffering and crucifixion from a very early period. Isaiah 53's innovative idea that an innocent person's suffering could substitute for that of the guilty, using language used elsewhere for making atonement with God for sin through sacrifice (Isa 53:10, compare Lev 5:6, etc.), became the key prooftext for the gospel writers' image of Jesus as the sacrificial 'Lamb of God' who takes away sin (John 1:29, 36; 1 Pet 1:18–19; Rev 5:6; 7:14). Paul used the passage to explain atonement by identifying Jesus as the one 'who was handed over to death for our trespasses and was raised for our justification' (Rom 4:22–25, compare 2 Cor 5:21; 1 Cor 15:3–4), while Jesus uses Isa 53:13 ("he was numbered with the transgressors") to portray himself as a political radical (Luke 22:35–37; Matt 10:34). Elsewhere in the New Testament, Paul uses the opening verses (52:14–53:1) to emphasize the importance of spreading the gospel (Rom 10:14–17); John 12:36–38 uses Isa 53:1 to explain the disciples' failure to believe, despite all the signs that Jesus had performed in their presence; and Matt 8:14–17 understands Jesus's healings as fulfilling Isa 53:4. Foreshadowing the chapter's significance in the history of Christian evangelism, in Acts 8:26–38 an Ethiopian eunuch reads Isa 53:7–8 and asks to be baptized.

In the end, these 'servant songs' are probably better understood within the wider context of Second Isaiah, rather than in isolation. Servant language appears repeatedly in Second Isaiah, and the variety of individual and community entities to which ʿebed refers in these texts suggests a multivalent term that has been put to multiple uses by the Isaianic author(s) (41:8–10; 42:18–20; 43:8–10; 44:1–5, 21, 24–28; 45:1–4; 48:20; 54:17).

With this in mind, the use of *'ebed* elsewhere in the Hebrew Bible is especially illuminating. The term is frequently used to describe Yнwн's most faithful followers, including Abraham (Gen 18; Exod 32:13; Deut 9:27; Ps 105), Isaac (Exod 32:13; Deut 9:27), Jacob (Gen 32; Deut 9:27; Ezek 28:25), Caleb (Num 14:24), Moses (Exod 4; 14; Num 11; Deut 34; Josh 1; etc.), David (1 Kgs 8:66; Isa 37:35; Jer 33:21, 26; Ezek 34:23–24; 37:24–25; Pss 78; 89 etc.) and Job (Job 1:8; 2:3; 42:7–8). By extension, it can also be used of the people of Israel as a whole (e.g. Lev 25; Deut 32; Jer 30:10; 46:27–28; Ps 136:22); this is, by a narrow margin, its most common use in Isa 40–55.

As an expression of particular intimacy between a person and Yнwн, *'ebed* was also a natural way of describing the relationship between Yнwн and Yнwн's prophets. This is especially common in the Deuteronomistic literature, which has a particular interest in the role of the prophets in communicating divine displeasure to the people prior to judgement (2 Kgs 9:7; 17:13; Jer 7:25; 25:4; 26:5; 35:15; 44:4; Ezek 38:17; Am 3:7; Zech 1:6; Dan 9:6, 10; Ezr 9:11.) It is also used of several individual prophets, including Isaiah (Isa 20:3), Elijah (2 Kgs 10:10), Ahijah (1 Kgs 14:18) and Jonah (2 Kgs 14:25). Isaiah 40–55 has a number of characteristics that suggest an awareness of this wider Deuteronomistic tradition. Two early references to Yнwн's servant, in particular, use *'ebed* as a metonym for 'prophet' in passages that emphasize the role of the prophets as crucial witnesses to divine foreknowledge (42:10; 44:26), although whom they have in mind is somewhat ambiguous. The Hebrew text of Isa 44:26 uses the singular *'ebed*, raising the possibility that Yнwн (the speaker) is referring to a specific prophet; some of the versions, however, use a more generic plural ('prophets'), paralleling the plural 'messengers' that follows. Isaiah 42:10 is similar; the text was read by the Masoretic scribes as singular – but the same consonants could also be taken as a plural. The plural appears also in Isa 54:17, where it describes the inhabitants of Jerusalem and broadens the intimate relationship with Yhwh to the whole people. This is in keeping with the immediately following text, where the covenant once made with David is extended to the whole people.

The second half of Second Isaiah much more clearly uses the singular *'ebed* to refer to the anonymous prophet who stands behind Second Isaiah (49:1–6; 50:4–11; 52:13–13:12). Three of the four original 'servant songs' – including Isa 53 – appear in this part of Second Isaiah. The first speaks of Yнwн's choice of the prophet prior even to his birth, echoing similar language in Jeremiah (49:1; cf. Jer 1:4). Both chapters liken the prophet to a military armoury, metaphorically girding them up to face the opposition of their people (Isa 49:2; Jer 1:17–19). Both also describe the prophetic call in terms appropriate to the international atmosphere of their times; Jeremiah is appointed 'a prophet to the nations' (Jer 1:5), while the anonymous prophet of Second Isaiah will be 'a light to the nations' (Isa 49:6); the nations themselves are summoned to witness to this account of the prophet's call to YHWH's service (49:1). As the echoes of Jeremiah suggest, the use of 'ebed in these chapters is consonant with its use for individual prophets in the Deuteronomistic material (and for Isaiah ben Amoz in 20:3). Second Isaiah also has well-known and extensive links with the psalms, where 'ebed is used by dozens of anonymous supplicants to emphasize their relationship with YHWH. It is perhaps on a combination of these traditions that Second Isaiah relies when it speaks of its anonymous, prophetic figure as an 'ebed. In Isa 50:4–9 the first-person prophetic voice describes the opposition the speaker has encountered in his attempts to convey the divine word. Although this voice does not self-identify as YHWH's servant, the passage is immediately followed by a question to the people: 'Who among you fears YHWH, and obeys the voice of his servant?' (50:10). A similar phenomenon occurs in Isa 52:13–53:12, in which the servant is identified as such in the divine voice (52:13; 53:11) and the people's opposition to him is described at length by other, anonymous voices (53:1–10; cf. 49:7).

These latter passages, which speak of YHWH's servant in the third person, are also evidence that 'Second Isaiah' is a more complex, multi-layered collection than the simple nomenclature of 'Second Isaiah' initially suggests. Although the origins of this material seem to be with one or more anonymous prophetic figures in the sixth century, speaking to the diaspora in hope and expectation, the text is also quite clear that the prophet(s)'s message was received and annotated by the community to which it was addressed, as the people sought to understand what it had meant, and how it – and its deliverer – had been misunderstood. First Isaiah and prophetic books like Jeremiah attest to a similar phenomenon, in which oracular material that (one may suppose) originated with a prophetic individual prompted further reflection and elaboration once it had been committed to writing. Indeed, the interpretation of Isa 40–55 has increasingly recognized differing voices within these chapters, acknowledging this and other evidence for editorial activity. The distinction between Isa 40–48 and Isa 49–55 is the most significant and most widely acknowledged differentiation, but the extent of the editorial developments within these major sections is now a major topic of scholarly discussion. While 'First', 'Second' and 'Third' Isaiah remain useful as a chronological schematic, they are far from the whole story of the book of Isaiah.

Before moving on, one further usage of ʿ*ebed* in Second Isaiah is worth attention. As noted above, one of the theologically most significant uses of ʿ*ebed* elsewhere in the Hebrew Bible is for the Davidic king (1 Kgs 8:66; Isa 37:35; Jer 33:21, 26; Ezek 34:23–24; 37:24–25; Pss 78; 89 etc.). In a blow to Davidic expectations of unceasing divine favour, Jeremiah used the term for Nebuchadnezzar, the Babylonian king, in order to articulate the legitimacy of Nebuchadnezzar's actions as judgement against Yʜwʜ's people: the term is a sign of Yʜwʜ's relationship with the foreign king and Yʜwʜ's use of him in bringing about Yʜwʜ's own ends (Jer 25:9; 27:6; 43:10). Second Isaiah takes this reimagining of Yʜwʜ's earthly ways and means one step farther, describing Yʜwʜ's new representative, Cyrus, as Yʜwʜ's chosen servant (42:1). The latter part of the chapter acknowledges the unconventionality of this arrangement: like Nebuchadnezzar, this servant of Yʜwʜ does not know Yʜwʜ (42:19–20). Nevertheless, the situation of the people is so dire that Yʜwʜ is prepared to make use of him anyway (42:22). Like the old Davidic kings, but now in lieu of them, Cyrus has been chosen by Yʜwʜ to bring about justice for the people (42:1, 3–4).

This internationalized perspective on Yʜwʜ's engagement with the world is one of Second Isaiah's most notable contributions to the theology of the Hebrew Bible. Prior to the exile, Yʜwʜ had been conceived primarily as Israel's national deity. Although First Isaiah depicts Yʜwʜ using other nations to inflict punishment upon Israel and Judah, and thus implicitly presupposes Yʜwʜ's authority beyond the homeland of his own people, the Israelite homeland and the people in it were the primary focus of Yʜwʜ's attention; foreign nations were of interest only insofar as their fates intersected with Israel's. With the demise of the kingdoms and the dispersal of their inhabitants, the once-tight connection between Yʜwʜ and Israel as a national-territorial entity gave way to a more global perspective. The people were scattered to the four corners of the earth, and they wondered: Could Yʜwʜ intervene on their behalf, even in distant lands? Or were Yʜwʜ's powers outside their traditional homeland limited by the powers of the native gods?

The forced internationalization of Yʜwʜ's people in the sixth century thus gave the biblical authors a wider perspective on the extent of Yʜwʜ's worldwide rule – and, as a corollary, the first inklings that a more expansive definition of the Yahwistic community might be possible. Eventually this would lead to a shift away from a strictly ethnic conception of 'Israel', towards a more religiously conceived one. Second Isaiah already signals that Yʜwʜ's intentions extend far beyond the limited, nationalist vision of a single nation or people (55:8–9), and imagines unknown strangers turning towards Israel's God (55:5); Third Isaiah, as the next chapter will explore, takes this idea even further.

Second Isaiah's concern to preach salvation to the Israelite diaspora nevertheless provokes some quite negative statements regarding the nations. These arise in part as an element of the emphasis on the exclusivity of YHWH's power over world events. If YHWH is in control, then the powers of the nations – even the most formidable of empires – are inconsequential. 'All the nations are as nothing before him; they are accounted by him as less than nothing and emptiness' (40:17; cf. 43:4).

These negative statements about the nations also arise as a response to Israelite suffering at foreigners' hands: many died in the siege of Jerusalem, or on the forced marches to Babylonia. Those who survived lived under Babylonian imperial authority for decades. The humiliation of Jerusalem's defeat was enabled by the treachery of Egypt and other allies who failed to come to its aid (2 Kgs 24:7), and exacerbated by the perfidy of the Edomites, who turned their backs on their Israelite brothers and took advantage of their weakness (Obad; Ps 137; Jer 49:7–22; Ezek 25:12–14). A certain gleeful delight at the prospect that these nations will soon be obliged to recognize YHWH's authority and the special status of YHWH's people is understandable under such circumstances: 'Kings shall be your foster fathers, and their queens your nursing mothers; with their faces to the ground they shall bow down to you, and lick the dust of your feet' (49:23; cf. 41:2; 45:1; 54:3).

Isaiah 55, the final chapter of Second Isaiah and a rhetorical hinge linking it to Third Isaiah, demonstrates Second Isaiah's ambivalence regarding the nations. On the one hand, the chapter signals a forthcoming shift in the nature of the Davidic covenant that makes it far more inclusive than previously imagined. Traditionally, YHWH's royal covenant was with the Davidic kings, who served as the mediating fulcrum of the relationship between YHWH and Israel. Now, YHWH is Israel's king. The covenant is thus no longer with the human king alone but directly with the people. The people, in turn, are to serve as the mediators between YHWH and the nations:

> I will make with you an everlasting covenant,
>   my steadfast, sure love for David.
> See, I made him a witness to the peoples.
> See, you shall call nations that you do not know,
>   and nations that do not know you shall run to you,
> because of YHWH your God,
>   the Holy One of Israel,
>   for he has glorified you. (55:3–5; cf. 49:6)

On the international scale on which Second Isaiah envisions Yhwh's activity occurring, Yhwh's special people have a special role in the salvation of all humanity. This marks a significant transition in Israelite identity: from a geographically based identity tied to the cultural and political realities of national territory to a more geographically fluid community bound together by the confession that Yhwh is God.

This does not mean a complete geographical or ethnic unmooring, however; while Second Isaiah's vision of the Yahwistic community is much broader than that previously envisioned, it remains oriented towards Jerusalem, and Israel retains its unique relationship with Yhwh. Nevertheless, it opens the door to the even greater expansiveness of Third Isaiah and the incorporation of proselytes into the Second Temple Jewish community (Isa 56, cf. Leviticus); much later, it will form part of the justification for the early Christian community's mission to the Gentiles (Acts 15 etc.).

Further reading

Barstad, Hans M. *The Babylonian Captivity of the Book of Isaiah: 'Exilic' Judah and the Provenance of Isaiah 40–55*. Oslo: Novus, 1997.

Boda, Mark J., Carol J. Dempsey and LeAnn S. Flesher, eds. *Daughter Zion: Her Portrait, Her Response*. Atlanta, GA: Society of Biblical Literature, 2012.

Darr, Katheryn Pfisterer. *Isaiah's Vision and the Family of God*. Louisville, KY: Westminster John Knox, 1994.

Laato, Antti. *Who Is the Servant of the Lord? Jewish and Christian Interpretations on Isaiah 53 from Antiquity to the Middle Ages*. Winona Lake, IN: Eisenbrauns, 2013.

O'Brien, Julia M. *Challenging Prophetic Metaphor: Theology and Ideology in the Prophets*. Louisville, KY: Westminster John Knox, 2008.

Schipper, Jeremy. *Disability and Isaiah's Suffering Servant*. Oxford: Oxford University Press, 2011.

Tiemeyer, Lena-Sofia. *For the Comfort of Zion: The Geographical and Theological Location of Isaiah 40–55*. Leiden: Brill, 2011.

Tull Willey, Patricia. *Remember the Former Things: The Recollection of Previous Texts in Second Isaiah*. Atlanta, GA: Scholars, 1997.

Williamson, H. G. M. *The Book Called Isaiah: Deutero-Isaiah's Role in Composition and Redaction*. Oxford: Oxford University Press, 1994.

4

Isaiah in the fifth century

The book of Isaiah reached something quite close to its final form in the fifth century BCE. This phase saw the addition of several chapters at the end of the book (Isa 56–66) as well as some final additions and re-workings of material elsewhere (especially Isa 1, which brings together material from a number of different periods to provide an introductory framework for the entire book). Like Isa 40–55, these oracles and poems are anonymous, although these authors likewise present their work as an extension of the Isaianic tradition, appending it to the older Isaianic materials while alluding to and re-using elements from those earlier traditions.

Historical contexts

The historical context of Isa 56–66 is not easy to discern. Unlike the material associated with Isaiah ben Amoz in the eighth century, or the chapters linked to the anonymous prophet of the sixth century, the last eleven chapters of the book of Isaiah lack clear historical referents. They refer to no kings, foreign or domestic, nor any wars, earthquakes, or natural phenomena that might locate their remarks historically. They do not even mention the name of the era's major imperial power, Persia. Moreover, although quite a lot is now known of Persian politics and policy, this knowledge focuses on the Persian heartland; much remains uncertain regarding the situation on the ground in distant provinces like Yehud.

Furthermore, these chapters are probably not the product of a single, concentrated moment in history, such that pinning down the context of one passage would provide a solid footing for the rest. Instead, the concerns of this material suggest changing social and political circumstances over many years, perhaps even several decades. Among the most notable evidence for this lengthy historical timeline concerns the temple, which appears sometimes to be still in ruins (64:11), but elsewhere to be rebuilt and a focus of community disagreement (66:6; perhaps 56:7). Whether these chapters represent the compiled efforts of a single author working over a long career, or are the work of several authors, is unknown. The contrasting viewpoints they contain perhaps suggest that the latter is more likely.

Sketching the historical background behind this final phase of the book of Isaiah is thus an exercise in broad brushstrokes. Chapters 60–62, generally considered the earliest material contained in Third Isaiah, date perhaps to the end of the sixth century, shortly before the second temple was completed in 515. The latest parts of the surrounding material probably date to the middle of the fifth century, around the time of Ezra and Nehemiah. This is suggested especially by references in Isa 66 to those who 'tremble' at the word of God, using an unusual word (*haredim*) that is used in this sense elsewhere only in Ezr 9–10. These 'tremblers' seem to have been a sectarian subgroup within the Persian Period Judean community, differentiated from the wider community in the context of a crisis over the community's boundaries. The prevalence of related concerns in Isa 56–66 suggests that parts of Third Isaiah were occasioned by a similar context.

In its entirety, however, Third Isaiah addresses an era after some of those whom Second Isaiah summoned to migrate to Jerusalem had taken up the challenge to settle in the homeland. Thus, unlike Second Isaiah, which vacillates between the homeland and the diaspora, Third Isaiah is consistently concerned with matters in the homeland.

The situation there was far from rosy. Although it was not the 'empty land' that some biblical texts depict (e.g. Isa 6:12; 2 Kgs 25:11), the cities and towns of Judah had suffered badly from the kingdom's defeat. The exact state of Jerusalem after 586 is not fully understood, but it is clear that the Babylonians had destroyed the temple (2 Kgs 25:9 // Jer 52:13; Lam 2:1–7) and that the provincial administration was indefinitely relocated to Mizpah (Jer 40–41). Attempts to reckon the overall damage inflicted on Judah's population are inevitably guesswork, but perhaps as much as 80 percent of the population was deported or died as a result of the wars. Those who were left appear to have reverted to subsistence farming, with little time and few resources left over for rebuilding efforts in the larger towns and cities. There are some indications that lamentation and other liturgical practices were sustained at the site of the temple while it lay in ruins (Jer 41:4–5; Lamentations), but the city surrounding it remained small and impoverished for many years. Even in the fifth century the people are said to have drawn lots to determine who would have to live in the city (Neh 11:1–2). Give how little it had to offer them, it is hardly surprising that few wanted to move there.

Life in Yehud – the name by which the former kingdom of Judah was known once it was provincialized – under the Persians was nevertheless somewhat better than it had been under the Babylonians. Persian policy appears to have favoured local governance arrangements, rather than seeking to impose Persian law throughout the empire, so it seems likely that the population in Yehud was permitted a degree of autonomy – provided that they supported the empire and its king. Unfortunately, there is no direct evidence from the Persian side regarding imperial policy in the southern Levant, and the historical value of the administrative material preserved in Ezra–Nehemiah is uncertain. Evidence from Egypt and elsewhere, however, suggests that Persian officials encouraged the codification of local legal traditions, which were then adopted as imperial policy in the area. A similar process may have provided the impetus for the compilation of Israelite legal traditions in the form of the Pentateuch, though undoubtedly there were other factors at work as well.

Exactly how far the jurisdiction of these laws might have extended is not clear. Although Yehud had its own governor for much of the period, it was always part of a much larger administrative unit. Initially this was a very large Persian satrapy comprising formerly Babylonian territories that included southern Mesopotamia and most of the Levant, but in the mid-fifth century this was divided and Yehud was left within the Levantine region of Eber-Nari ('Beyond the [Euphrates] River'). Within these larger administrative structures, Ezra–Nehemiah reports strained relations between the governors of Yehud and those of surrounding territories, especially Samaria. Yehud may at one time have been under the direct authority of the governor at Samaria, though this is not certain. The names of a number of governors in Jerusalem are moreover preserved in biblical and extra-biblical sources, which suggests a degree of local authority independent of decisions in Samaria.

The territory controlled by these governors continued to be relatively impoverished throughout much of the period; even after some of the descendants of the people deported from the city in 597 and 586 returned to live there, the city remained a small one. Ezra 2:64 and Neh 7:66 give 42,360 as the population of citizens in the whole province, not counting slaves and others, but it may have been substantially less. The prophetic book of Haggai blames delays in the rebuilding of the temple on the people's lack of will, but also admits that eking out a living in the province was proving exceptionally difficult, and that there was not much time or energy left over for temple-building (Hag 1:6, cf. 2:7–8). The visions of Zech 1–8 likewise reveal the poverty of Jerusalem and its inhabitants, as they dream of a more glorious future (Zech 1:17; 2:4; 8:4–6). Both books date their oracles to 520, the second year of Darius and nearly two decades after Cyrus led the Persians onto the global stage. The prophets' frustrations reflect the privations suffered by those living in a provincial backwater, where there was never enough to eat or drink, let alone funds to spare for building projects (Hag 1:6). The silver and gold that were to be found came largely from those still living abroad (Zech 6:10-11). Ezra and Nehemiah also describe slow-moving building projects, artfully intermingling reports of delays in rebuilding the temple with reports of setbacks in rebuilding the city walls, and seeking to blame both on interventions by Yehud's neighbours (Ezr 3–6; Neh 2; 4; 6).

The reality of Persian-period Yehud, then, was a far cry from the glorious restoration promised by Isa 40–55 (cf. Ezek 33–48). Expectations for the return had been high – bounteous crops and flocks, numerous offspring, and Jerusalem rebuilt with precious jewels (Isa 55). Reality was a disappointment: a pale imitation of the glorious restoration envisioned by the likes of Second Isaiah and Ezekiel. The city walls whose reconstruction was stymied in Nehemiah are also in ruins in Isa 60:10; the sanctuary lies desolate, burnt to the ground, in Isa 63:18 and 64:11. This gap between prophetic vision and provincial reality required explanation. Why, after such excitement and promise by Second Isaiah and others, had reality fallen so short? Much of Isa 56–66 is an attempt to explain the situation.

Theological themes and concerns

When the voices of Third Isaiah ask why Second Isaiah's promises of a glorious restoration had not yet been realized, their responses draw on the breadth and depth of the Isaianic tradition. As in the earlier layers of the book, Yhwh's character as superlatively holy, just and righteous is fundamental to the structure of the life of Yhwh's people. As representatives of their God, they must be holy, just and righteous, reflecting the superlative divine as nearly as humanly possible. According to Third Isaiah, it is the people's failure to pursue justice and righteousness, together with their persistent violations of Yhwh's holiness, that has impeded the realization of Yhwh's kingdom on earth.

Although these chapters are consistent with the older traditions in important ways, they also take them in new and sometimes surprising directions. The prophetic imagination is especially notable in cases concerning the delineation of the community's boundaries: who may, and who may not, be part of Yhwh's people. On the one hand, Third Isaiah's conception of the Yahwistic community expands beyond that of its predecessors, to include persons historically excluded from it, such as foreigners and eunuchs (Isa 56:1–8). At the same time, Third Isaiah insists more stringently on the importance of community members' behaviour, narrowing the parameters of the community to exclude even those who were born into it, if they fail to uphold its standards. The community envisioned by these chapters is thus one that is increasingly defined in religious and moral terms, with parentage granted less and less weight. This is why the people's failures vis-à-vis justice, righteousness and holiness are so problematic, and why they form such a recurring theme in Third Isaiah's explanations of the delay of the promised restoration.

At the heart of Third Isaiah are three chapters that offer a robust affirmation of the ongoing validity of Second Isaiah's promises of restoration (Isa 60–62). Because of their similarity to Isa 40–55, Isa 60–62 is often considered the oldest material preserved within Third Isaiah; some have even argued that this section should be understood as displaced material belonging to Second Isaiah. Certainly, as Ulrich Berges and others have pointed out, the once-hard-and-fast division of Second and Third Isaiah at the beginning of Isa 56 has been complicated by the recognition of multiple voices within each of these major sections.

At its centre, Isa 61 offers a brief glimpse of a first-person speaker who self-identifies in terms very similar to those used to described Yhwh's servant in Second Isaiah: 'Yhwh has anointed me; he has sent me to bring good news to the oppressed, to bind up the broken-hearted, to proclaim liberty to the captives, and release to the prisoners' (61:1; compare 42:1, 6–7; 49:6, 9). Insofar as it is possible to speak of Third Isaiah as a discrete individual, these three chapters are the ones most plausibly conceived as this anonymous prophet's work, around which Isa 56–66 later grew.

As in Isa 40–55, Jerusalem's coming glory is the main focus. The nations have showered Jerusalem with verbal abuse, declaring that the city must have been 'Abandoned' and 'Deserted' by its God (62:4). As Mark Gray and others have noted, the destruction of Jerusalem, the deportation of many of its inhabitants, and the suffering of its survivors had raised serious questions about Yhwh's character and commitment to justice. These chapters admit that previous generations saw powerful nations overshadow the city and deport her inhabitants, but insist that Jerusalem's glory will shine again, with such brightness that all the nations will see it, because its 'light has come!' (60:1). This echoes the imperatives to Jerusalem to 'Rise up!' from its earlier suffering (51:17). In the coming age, the city will be called the 'City That Is Not Abandoned' and be recognized as the one of whom YHWH has declared, 'My Delight Is in Her' (62:4, 12). This extension of divine comfort to those who lament seeks to vindicate YHWH's character, affirming that YHWH remains a God committed to justice (61:2–3). The promise of a double portion (61:7) similarly recalls the announcement that Jerusalem had 'received from the YHWH's hand double for all her sins' (40:2) and seeks to reassure the audience of YHWH's perfect justice.

The gifts and tribute brought to the city by the nations (who now stand completely in awe of Zion, rather than mocking it) are destined for the temple. There, despite their wealth, they will pale in comparison to the glory of the Holy One of Israel (60:5–7, 9). Indeed, the honour and riches that the nations will bring to Jerusalem are not a response to the city's or its inhabitants' merit. Rather, they are a response to the presence of YHWH in the temple on Mount Zion and a recognition of YHWH's glory. That said, these two things are not entirely unrelated. The metaphors of sight and blindness that earlier parts of the book used to signal the people's response (or lack thereof) to YHWH's desire for justice here signal that the purpose of YHWH's actions is to fill Jerusalem with righteousness (62:1; compare 6:10; 29:9, 18; 35:5; 42:7, 16, 18–19; 43:8; 56:10). The light that comes from YHWH is a light that overcomes darkness, with liberation as its aim (60:19–61:1). Both the people and the nations will see YHWH's light and respond appropriately.

As in Second Isaiah, YHWH's city is imagined metaphorically as a grief-stricken mother, bereaved of her children. But now Third Isaiah promises that Jerusalem's children, who have been held captive among the nations for a generation or more, will finally be freed to come home (60:4, 9; compare 49:20–25; 51:17–20; 54:1–2). This image of YHWH gathering the people from all the distant corners of the earth is picked up several times in other layers of Third Isaiah, including the prominent opening description of YHWH as the one 'who gathers the outcasts of Israel' (56:8; compare 57:14).

This element of YHWH's activity makes good sense in the late sixth and fifth centuries. Some of the deportees' descendants in Babylonia had returned to Yehud, but many had not yet done so; other YHWH-worshippers were in Egypt, descended from a group of refugees who had fled there after the fall of Judah; still others had survived scattered across the Levant. Indeed, the sixth-century migrations resulting from the kingdom's destruction created a diaspora people that persists even today. Then as now, many hoped that eventually all of Yhwh's people would make their way back to the homeland. Third Isaiah's declaration that Yhwh would continue to gather in his people, until all have returned, witnesses to a hope kindled by Cyrus but still unfulfilled.

Despite Yhwh's positive desires for Jerusalem and Zion (62:10–12; 65:18–19), Third Isaiah argues that the people have repeatedly failed to hold up their end of the bargain (65:1–7). Israel's earlier prophets had also railed against the people's propensity to worship other gods, as well as their proclivity for ignoring Yhwh's commandments regarding right behaviour. Judgement was the inevitable result; neither Yhwh's reputation nor Yhwh's commitment to justice could tolerate such offences indefinitely. After the catastrophic judgements of the early sixth century, resulting in the kingdom's destruction and the people's dispersion, these prophets had concluded that Israel's relationship with Yhwh could no longer depend on the people's ability to keep Yhwh's commandments as in the Mosaic covenant. The only way forward was an 'everlasting' or 'eternal' covenant (Jer 32:40; Ezek 16:60; 37:26; compare Jer 31:31–34; 33:20–22).

Within the book of Isaiah, this idea is first mentioned in Isa 24:5, but it is taken up again in Isa 55:3, which forms a bridge between Second and Third Isaiah. The core of Third Isaiah then confirms the significance of this notion going forward, with Yhwh promising the surviving diaspora community a 'perpetual covenant' (*bᵉrît ôlam*, 61:8). The Hebrew *ôlam* connotes duration at the limits of human ability to conceive: thus will be the persistence of Yhwh's commitment to the people. Isaiah 59 makes a similar point, promising that Yhwh's spirit will never depart from the people or their descendants (59:21). As scholars such as Jacob Stromberg and Risto Nurmela have observed, the authors of Third Isaiah are constantly in conversation with the earlier Isaianic materials, interpreting them for and re-applying them in new situations.

The everlasting covenant is designed to be immutable in the face of human failing, but is not to be confused with permission for the people to act however they like. Every reference to Yhwh's covenant in Third Isaiah is clearly connected to Yhwh's (and the people's) righteousness. Thus, Isa 61:10 describes the people as 'clothed with the garments of salvation … covered with the robe of righteousness', while Isa 59:21 forms the climax of a depiction of Yhwh as acting to ensure the justice the people are failing to achieve (59:15b–19). Yhwh's promise of an everlasting covenant is thus a declaration of Yhwh's ongoing determination to see justice and righteousness fulfilled among the people.

Instead of punishment for misbehaviour, Yhwh swears that he will delight in Jerusalem perpetually, as a young man delights in his bride (62:5). The background is a metaphor employed by several of the prophets, in which the people's loyalty to Yhwh is likened to a woman's loyalty to her husband, and their disloyalty is akin to adultery (Hos 1–3; Jer 3; Ezek 16; 23). Isaiah 57 depicts the people's religious behaviour as an elaborate seduction scene. In Isa 62, however, the land of Judah is referred to as a married woman (62:4 compare 49:18; 54:5–6), reversing the older, negative uses of the marriage metaphor, as when Yhwh declared that Israel 'is not my wife, and I am not her husband' (Hos 2:2) or 'sent Israel away with divorce papers' (Jer 3:8). As in Isa 40–55, the divorce between Yhwh and the people is denied and forgotten (62:4; compare 50:1; 54:4-8). The city will be beloved and full of joyous children again (62:4, compare 49:19–22; 54:1–3).

Elements of this metaphor worked better in an ancient, patriarchal culture than they do today, insofar as the metaphor is based on problematic assumptions about gender roles and a patriarchal imbalance of power between husband and wife that is generally rejected by these texts' contemporary readers in Europe and North America. The metaphor continues to function positively where it foregrounds the extreme care expected of each party in a marital relationship; in Isa 62, Jerusalem is told to lobby Yhwh insistently – 'give (God) no rest'! (62:6) – if she is not treated with honour and respect. The metaphor is much more problematic when it depicts Yhwh as a chronically abusive spouse, vacillating alternating between violence and affection. Notably, Third Isaiah looks to draw a line under such inconstancy: Isa 62 recasts the violent history between Yhwh and Jerusalem as a tragic interlude that will never be repeated (in 62:8, Yhwh swears this by his right hand, a solemn oath formula).

Another striking aspect of Third Isaiah's vision, laid out already in these core chapters, is its breadth of perspective with regard to the nations. Although the earlier parts of Isaiah evidence a belief in Yhwh's authority over the whole earth, including the kings and peoples of other nations, Third Isaiah envisions these foreign peoples as potentially involved in the worship of Yhwh: as an integral part of the Yahwistic community, rather than merely subject to Yhwh's authority. Thus Jerusalem's light will attract people from other nations (60:4, 10–11, compare 66:18), and its orientation towards Yhwh will be the source of international justice (Isa 61).

A nationalist reading of this material might view it in triumphalist terms, with a downtrodden people longing for the subordination of other nations and peoples to Jerusalemite domination: the 'foreigners will rebuild your walls, and their kings will serve you' (60:10). But the thrust of the passage is suffused with a vision of justice that disallows such abuses of power. Where Second Isaiah emphasized the nations' subservience to Israel (49:23), Third Isaiah imagines one of equal inclusion. The exertion of dominance that once characterized the nations' attitudes will no longer hold: the foreigners who destroyed Jerusalem's walls will atone by rebuilding them, and those who believed that they ought to be served by others will heed the call to serve others themselves (60:10). There will be no more violence (60:18).

This vision – one of expansive inclusiveness regardless of former status – becomes more and more pronounced as Third Isaiah develops. Those who had been the least – the poor, the lowly, the weak, with whom Yhwh most identifies (56:3–7; 57:15) – will find their tormentors at their feet seeking forgiveness (60:13). Jerusalem will stand at the centre of this new international equilibrium, because Yhwh's sanctuary – and the orientation of not only Jerusalem but of all the nations towards it – is the ultimate source of these renewed relations. The one true lord, the only one with a rightful claim to reign over humanity, is Yhwh.

The chapters around Isa 60–62 build on and continue many of these themes. This later material, drawing on but going beyond both Second Isaiah and Isa 60–62, makes clear that its own audience has also inherited the promises of Yhwh: first made in the mid-sixth century by Second Isaiah (Isa 40–55), reaffirmed in the late sixth century by the earliest parts of Third Isaiah (Isa 60–62), and now extended to the next generation. These latest voices come perhaps from the first half of the fifth century, down to around the time of Ezra (probably *c.* 458 BCE).

The continuity of the promise is conveyed especially through the use of terms and phrases that identify the current generation with the previous ones. Thus, Third Isaiah assures its audience that Yhwh is still 'your redeemer, the mighty one of Jacob' (60:16), who 'will feed you with the heritage of your ancestor Jacob' (58:14; also 58:1; 65:9). These references to Jacob echo Second Isaiah's references to the people as Jacob/Israel, and set the audience up to hear the promises made to the people by Second Isaiah as addressed to them as well (40:27; 41:8 etc.). The audience is also described as Yhwh's 'servants' (63:17; 65:8–9, 13–15; 66:14), recalling the extensive servant language in Second Isaiah and using that language to identify the present community as the inheritors of Yhwh's chosen servant (49:1–7;

50:4–11; 52:13–53:12). The emphasis on 'servants', rather than on a singular 'servant', suggests that Yʜwʜ's revelation is no longer mediated through a single member of the community. Now, all members of the community are servants – though the community is also more restricted (see below).

Characterized as Yʜwʜ's servants and the heirs of Jacob, Third Isaiah's fifth-century audience stands in expectation of Yʜwʜ's promises of restoration: a glorious renewal of Jerusalem's glory and the triumphal return of the people to Zion, where the foreign nations will bow down to them (Isa 40–55; 60–62). Yet, decades after the reign of Cyrus and the first wave of migrants to Yehud, this restoration was still not forthcoming.

The remaining chapters of Third Isaiah identify lapses in ethical behaviour as the reason for the delay. It opens with a summons to 'Maintain justice, and do what is right' (56:1). Although the people say they want the benefits of a relationship with Yʜwʜ – namely, a divinely protected city that is the nations' envy – they have been unwilling to act in a way that facilitates, or even is appropriate to, that relationship (58:1–9). Riven with injustice, the community has effectively inhibited Yʜwʜ's restorative presence and held off the restoration.

The call to justice was not new: similar exhortations occur throughout the biblical traditions, especially in the prophetic literature, and are prominent throughout Isaiah. The Song of the Vineyard identified bloodshed in place of justice and cries of oppression in lieu of righteousness as the cause of the people's destruction (5:7; compare 10:2; 28:17). In Isa 40–55, the foremost responsibility of Yʜwʜ's servant was to 'bring forth justice' in Israel and the nations (42:1, 3–4; compare 51:1, 4).

Isaiah 56–66 takes up these traditions with gusto, reinforcing the connection between Yʜwʜ's character and Yʜwʜ's moral expectations regarding the people: They are supposed to do what is right, because Yʜwʜ's salvation and righteousness are 'coming soon' (56:1). Jerusalem's continuing dereliction is the fault of the people for their inability to act justly and do what is righteous, not the fault of Yʜwʜ for failing to follow through on earlier promises.

The problems these chapters identify are portrayed in extreme terms, and indeed Third Isaiah may have taken a degree of rhetorical licence in order to get the point across. The people are not only failing to act righteously (Isa 58) – sins of omission – but actively pursuing wickedness: 'your lips speak lies; your tongues mutter malice… no one pleads truthfully… speaking deceit' (59:3–4). The social rot is comprehensive, infecting not only Israel's leaders (56:10–12) but the community as a whole (59:12–15). So many of the people are working actively against justice and eschewing righteous behaviour that the prophet can declare that 'justice is far' and 'righteousness beyond our reach' (59:9).

It is clear from these texts that doing justice and acting righteously are not merely general virtues, towards which the people are to strive in an abstract sense. Rather, they require specific action: the people are to welcome the immigrant and the disabled into the community as full and equal members, for example (56:3–8).

Although the connection between virtue and action is deeply rooted in the biblical tradition, these specific orders may have been quite shocking to Third Isaiah's original audience. Ezekiel 44:6–9 identifies the admission of foreigners into the temple as one of the causes of Judah's destruction and the people's deportation, and Deut 23:2 prohibits any male whose genitalia have been damaged from entering YHWH's sanctuary. Isaiah 56 challenges the perpetual validity of such exclusiveness, declaring that 'the eunuchs who keep my sabbaths, choose what I desire, and remain loyal to my covenant' (56:4) and 'the immigrants who have joined to YHWH, serving him and loving his name' (56:4) will be accepted by YHWH when they approach the most sacred precincts of YHWH's temple in Jerusalem (56:7).

The name of the modern State of Israel's Holocaust museum, Yad VaShem, is an allusion to this passage, specifically Isa 56:5 ('I will give, in my house and within my walls, a monument and a name [*yad vashem*]'). The Hebrew text of the verse is displayed in towering letters on the wall of a courtyard, as a promise to remember those who were killed, especially those who had no surviving offspring to remember them.

Third Isaiah is adamant that a demonstrated commitment to divine justice is more important as a measure of membership in YHWH's community than whether someone can prove that their parents and grandparents were Israelite before them. As Joseph Blenkinsopp has argued, the term 'servants' is especially prominent in passages that seek to differentiate members of the community whose behaviour marks them out as YHWH's faithful servants from those whose behaviour suggests otherwise. This redefinition of the boundaries of YHWH's community – from one determined largely in terms of ethnic descent to one defined primarily by religious praxis – is one of the most significant innovations of Third Isaiah.

Other texts from the Persian period suggest that debates over group boundaries were an ongoing issue. Among other factors, these arguments were provoked by differences between those whose ancestors had been deported to Babylonia and those who remained in the homeland, as well as increased contact with foreigners from other parts of the empire. Third Isaiah's inclusive attitude contrasts sharply with Ezra–Nehemiah, in which descent from persons deported to Babylonia is considered critical to membership in the restored community, described as the 'holy seed' (Ezr 9:2). Both Ezra and Nehemiah record efforts to remove those who cannot prove such descent from the community (Ezr 9–10; Neh 13). Third Isaiah is more in keeping with the Book of Ruth, in which a Moabite woman is incorporated into the genealogy of King David (Ruth 4:13–22). Ruth is often seen as an implicit critique of the exclusivism of Ezra and Nehemiah.

Third Isaiah's remarks about the sabbath (56:2, 6; 58:13; 66:23) and worship in the temple (56:5–7; 66:1–6) suggest that its ideas about Yhwh's justice and righteousness were closely linked to ideas about Yhwh's holiness. There are two components of this issue that are useful to distinguish. First, the people must maintain certain standards of holiness in order to be near Yhwh, because Yhwh is superlatively holy (compare Lev 11:44–45; 19:2; 20:26; 21:8, 'you shall be holy for I am holy'). The reader of the book of Isaiah has encountered this idea already, when Isaiah of Jerusalem expressed his anxiety about being in the presence of the 'holy, holy, holy Yhwh of Hosts' (6:3–5). The people's failure to maintain the ritual purity necessary to this kind of holiness also featured prominently in Ezekiel's explanation for Jerusalem's destruction: the people had so defiled Jerusalem that Yhwh had to leave the city, and without divine protection it fell quickly to the Babylonian invaders (Ezek 11:22–23).

Secondly, Yhwh's holiness has moral implications, because it is linked to Yhwh's commitments to justice and righteousness. This connection is also deeply rooted in the Isaianic tradition; Isaiah of Jerusalem repeatedly identified the people's failures of justice and righteousness as affronts to Yhwh's holiness (e.g. 5:15–16). In Third Isaiah's time, this association of Yhwh's holiness with justice and righteousness is why Third Isaiah can say that Yhwh will not only 'dwell in the high and holy place,' but 'also with those who are contrite and humble in spirit' (57:15). The word that Third Isaiah uses for 'crushed' is the same that Second Isaiah used to describe the suffering servant in Isa 53:5. Both passages assert that Yhwh has a special solidarity with the suffering and marginalized. The God of the universe is present alongside the powerless, pursuing justice on their behalf. Imitation of God (*imitatio Dei*) is a core principle of Third Isaiah's theological ethics.

Herein lies the Jerusalemites' problem. Instead of seeking justice for those abused by the powerful, as Yhwh does, the people are putting on shows of piety and pursuing violence among themselves (58:3–4). Put another way: they go through the motions of religious observance, maintaining the ritual holiness they think is required for proximity to Yhwh, but have missed the substance of what it means to be a Yhwh-follower, namely, to act on behalf of the marginalized in defence of justice (58:3, 13). Maintaining ritual holiness via meticulously correct worship practices is not meaningless, but it cannot make up for failures of justice and righteousness. Some of the people are reportedly so obsessed with superficial piety that they warn others to 'Keep to yourself, do not come near me, for I am too holy for you!' (65:5). This concern for holiness at all costs has made it idolatrous.

Warnings about the limitations of institutionalized worship are another of Third Isaiah's characteristic concerns. The issue comes to a climax at the end of the book, in a depiction of Yhwh as so great and so powerful that no earthly temple could possibly contain the divine majesty (Isa 66). The vision of Isaiah ben Amoz suggested that Yhwh was imagined to be so large that merely 'the hem of his robe filled the temple', but did not try to deny that Yhwh was present there (6:1; compare Yhwh as 'enthroned upon the cherubim', Exod 25:18–22; 35:7–8; 1 Kgs 7–8). Isaiah 66, by contrast, uses the limitations of temple architecture and an expansive creation theology to conclude that the temple is simply inadequate as an abode for Yhwh – even the entire earth is merely Yhwh's footstool (66:1–2). Accordingly, humility is more valuable to Yhwh than offerings and animal sacrifices made in the temple (66:2–3; compare Mic 6:6–8). Sacrifices are even described as burdensome to Yhwh, in a passage likely linked to Third Isaiah (1:10–17).

Third Isaiah's objections to the temple cult are declared in somewhat more extreme terms, but these prophetic protestations concerning empty religious rituals were not new. Amos professed Yhwh's hatred of offerings, when they were presented in the absence of justice and righteousness (Amos 5:21–25), and Jeremiah railed against reliance on religious ritual to blot out oppression and injustice (Jer 7). Indeed, as is typically the case with such passages, Third Isaiah does not in fact reject the temple wholesale; most notably, Isa 56:6–7 uses temple service to indicate the fullness of the foreigners' and eunuchs' inclusion in the community.

The problem is not with religious praxis *per se*; rather, it is an opposition to people who engage in the public performance of piety without enacting its corresponding substance. Yhwh is a God who cares for the poor, the homeless, and the mistreated. Yhwh's people demonstrate their commitment to Yhwh by enacting the values most central to Yhwh's character, not by placating the deity with offerings. If they are to worship Yhwh truly, the people must do these things as well (58:6–7, 9). Those who are unwilling to orientate their lives towards the pursuit of divine justice will discover that reliance on mindless rituals brings about catastrophe (65:11; 66:6).

One factor motivating this negativity concerning the temple was the reality of a persistent and far-flung diaspora. Already in the sixth century, prophets like Ezekiel and Second Isaiah had been forced to grapple with questions about YHWH's global authority. With faithful Yahwists scattered from Egypt to Persia, there had to be ways of approaching YHWH that did not require the temple, or even worshippers' presence in Jerusalem. An emphasis on private prayer and Torah study in other post-exilic texts is part of the tradition's response to this issue (compare Pss 1; 19; 51:15–17 [ET]). In making its own response, Third Isaiah is especially indebted to Second Isaiah's argument that, because YHWH was Creator of the entire universe, YHWH could act on Israel's behalf anywhere; nowhere was beyond YHWH's reach. Centuries later, Stephen would invoke Third Isaiah to defend a similarly expansive notion of divine presence in Acts 7.

One can infer that some sort of struggle between a group of Isaianic disciples and other members of the post-exilic community over access to and control over the temple precincts also motivated Third Isaiah's ambivalence about the temple cult. The exact nature of this dispute is elusive, but parts of Third Isaiah suggest significant divisions within the post-exilic community, as it insists that only those who adhere to the Isaianic line on key issues are chosen by YHWH for restoration (65:9, 15, 22). Those who engage in ritual fasting but neglect righteousness and justice, for example, will find that YHWH has turned away (58:2–7). Consistent with longstanding biblical ideologies, it also asserts that those who worship other deities with abhorrent practices will suffer and die (65:1–16).

This rhetoric is closely linked to Third Isaiah's distinctive definition of community boundaries, in which the happenstance of Israelite birth is not enough for inclusion in the restored community. Whereas promises of restoration in Second Isaiah were generally assumed to extend to Israel in its entirety (41:8–9 etc.), Third Isaiah concludes that only YHWH's (true) servants will enjoy divine blessing, and that these servants comprise only part of Israel as it had been traditionally conceived. This is most overt at the end of the book, where YHWH declares, in a series of powerful antitheses, that 'my servants shall eat, but you shall be hungry; my servants shall drink, but you shall be thirsty ... you shall leave your name to my chosen to use as a curse' (65:13–14).

Sociologically, this relentless rhetoric pitting 'my servants' against others in the post-exilic environment suggests that those in the Isaianic camp were out of power within the temple hierarchy. Deferring hope for justice into the afterlife, for example, is an attitude that tends to be adopted by those whose efforts to bring about change in the present have met with persistent failure (66:24; compare Dan 12:1–3). Third Isaiah's frustration with its community's earthly impotence, combined with its affirmations that God will see justice ultimately done, anticipate elements of apocalyptic thinking that are more fully developed in Daniel and Zechariah. Denied the practical means to effect change, Third Isaiah relies on fiery rhetoric: 'Those who tremble at [YHWH's] word' are assured that, though they face fierce opposition from those in power, 'your own people who hate you and reject you for my name's sake ... shall be put to shame' (66:5).

Despite the dismal outlook of present reality, Third Isaiah continues to affirm YHWH's commitment to justice and, in turn, to the people's eventual restoration. When Isa 63:7 announces an intention to praise YHWH for 'all YHWH did for us, for God's great favour toward the house of Israel', this is situated within a tradition that links praise of YHWH with confidence that YHWH will continue to act on the people's behalf. Isaiah 63 gives the exodus particular prominence, using YHWH's action in the past to summon YHWH to action in the present, on behalf of those who once again find themselves overpowered by their enemies (63:10–19; compare 64:3–4).

The same passage also acclaims YHWH as Israel's father (63:16; 64:8). Juxtaposed with acclamations of YHWH's power over all creation (63:15; 64:1–3, 8), this recalls the creation of humanity in Gen 1, in which the gift of the divine image signified YHWH's parental relationship with these new beings (Gen 1:26–27, compare 5:1–4). For Christians accustomed to speaking of YHWH as Father, such language may not register as unusual, but the depiction of YHWH in parental terms is especially associated with the post-exilic period (compare Mal 1:6, 10). YHWH is more reliable than forgetful human fathers. In a different familial metaphor, YHWH assumes the responsibility held by the '(kinsman-) redeemer' to rescue his people (63:16; compare Boaz's role in Ruth 4). This reprises a theme from Second Isaiah (47:4; 48:17, 20; 49:7, 26; 50:2; 51:10; 52:3, 9; 54:5, 8).

Elsewhere in the Hebrew Bible, appeals for YHWH to act on Israel's behalf rely on the idea that there is particular relationship between YHWH and Israel. Third Isaiah extends this relationship to non-Israelites who are prepared to worship YHWH, blurring the traditional boundaries between Israel and the nations. It also exhibits a clear conviction, inherited from the sixth-century Isaianic prophets, of Yhwh's universal authority over the whole of creation.

Parts of Third Isaiah's articulation of this universal Yahwistic vision rightly make modern readers uncomfortable. One of these is the scene of Yhwh's blood-soaked destruction of Edom (Isa 63). This is one of several oracles against Edom in prophetic texts from the sixth century or later (Ps 137; Jer 49:7–22; Ezek 25:12–14; Obad). Their unusual fury relates to the Edomites' involvement in the downfall of Jerusalem; the Edomites' exact crime is never fully explained, but the gist of the offence appears to have been an Edomite eagerness to take advantage of Judah's distress for its own gain (Ezek 35:5, 10). As Dominic S. Irudayaraj has observed, the gravity of this crime was heightened by the perceived family relationship between the Edomites and the Israelites (Gen 25). Elsewhere in Isaiah, another chapter that is probably contemporary with Third Isaiah declares that the Edomites are a people 'doomed to judgment' as a result (34:5). In Isa 63, the text is clear that vengeance upon the Edomites is Yhwh's doing alone; mere human beings must not arrogate to themselves the power of life and death. It is also clear, though lost in most translations, that Yhwh's intervention is motivated by the same moral commitments that drive much of Third Isaiah's rhetoric; the 'vindication' in Isa 63:1 uses the same word elsewhere translated 'righteousness' (*tsedeqah*).

Isaiah 59 brings out much more clearly the extent to which the divine character traits of justice and righteousness dominate Yhwh's interventions in the earthly realm, describing Yhwh as 'putting on righteousness as armour' in preparation for the divine reckoning (59:17). Although the juxtaposition of Yhwh as warrior and Yhwh as righteous judge may seem incongruous, in the ancient world both functions were closely connected to kingship (as the warrior-leaders in the book of Judges reflect). A good king was responsible for ensuring the welfare of his people, and this was achieved by protecting the realm from those who sought to invade and oppress it, by establishing the necessary mechanisms for justice, and then ensuring that they operated fairly. One of the psalmists offers a good summary of this ideal king: 'let the king bring justice to people who are poor, let him save the children of those who are needy, but let him crush oppressors … let the king rule from sea to sea, from the river to the ends of the earth' (Ps 72:4, 8). The human ideal is modelled on the divine king, Yhwh: what human kings aspired to, Yhwh actually does.

As Third Isaiah works its way towards its climactic vision of a fully realized new creation, Isa 65 invokes creation imagery familiar from Second Isaiah

(40:12; 42:5) as well as loyalty oath traditions familiar from Deuteronomy, signalling Yнwн's ongoing royal-divine pledge to care for and protect the people. Promises that the people 'will build houses and live in them; they will plant vineyards and eat their fruit' (65:21) directly annul curses found in Deuteronomy, where they depict the evil that would befall the Israelites when they failed to keep Yнwн's commandments. Similar curses appear in other ancient agreements, warning of the consequences for disloyalty. Judah's kings had sworn such oaths to the Babylonian kings; when they betrayed those oaths, Jerusalem was destroyed and the disasters inflicted upon it were understood as reprisals in keeping with curses laid out for disloyalty. Because those oaths were sworn in Yнwн's name, Jerusalem's destruction was also understood as a consequence of disloyalty to Yнwн (Ezek 17), and the devastation described with reference to the curses in Deuteronomy. The houses the people had built in Jerusalem and the vineyards planted in Judah were no use in Babylonia (Lam 5:2, compare Deut 28:30). Curses that spoke of horrifying acts of cannibalism by starving parents (Deut 28:53, 56–57) had come to pass (Lam 2:20; 4:10). Now, Isa 65 declares that these horrors are past. The new creation will be even more wonderful than the last – even the curse that humanity would labour for food will be overturned (65:23, compare Gen 3:7–8)!

A vision of Jerusalem in painless childbirth signals the radical departure of Yнwн's new creation from the realities of the old (66:7–8). The children are the city's inhabitants and their easy delivery is a sign of Jerusalem's renewed population. This excitement over a more populous future is coloured by frustration that fifth-century Jerusalem continued to be a shadow of its glory days as Judah's capital, when merchants and ambassadors from across the world came to bargain and trade. It also speaks to a context in which a town of a few tens of thousands of people would have been considered large; Babylon, the largest city in the ancient world, had a population of perhaps only 200,000. This was a very different context from today, when overpopulation and exhaustion of the planet's resources are among the most pressing global issues. The joy with which both Jerusalem and Yнwн greet the city's newest inhabitants contrasts with modern nation-states' lack of attention to the needs of their large urban populations: the satiation celebrated in Isa 66:11 is alien to the many hungry and homeless today.

The final verses of the book of Isaiah extend its vision as far as the mind can conceive. The centrality of the temple in Jerusalem as a sign of Yнwн's presence is renewed, as the delivery of people from all nations to Jerusalem is likened to offerings (66:20). That this is to be understood positively is clear from the promise to ordain some of these foreigners as priests and Levites (66:21). This final vision thus revisits and affirms the radically inclusive vision of Yhwh's people in Isa 56, in which foreigners and eunuchs were promised a full welcome into Yhwh's temple (56:3–8), bringing these chapters' – and the book's – vision of Yhwh's restored community to a climactic conclusion.

Again, the most important criterion for inclusion in Yhwh's 'new heavens and the new earth' is not ancestry but commitment to the worship of Yhwh (66:23) – even if it means travelling across the face of the earth, in whatever conveyance one can find, to do it. This willingness to look beyond the traditional boundaries of Israel for faithful worshippers of Yhwh is not a complete departure from earlier traditions' constructions of the Yahwistic community, but the point is certainly emphasized more here than elsewhere. Deuteronomy presumes that most Israelites will be such by birth, even as it acknowledges the possibility that those not born into the community might join it (Deut 23:7–8). It also recognizes the danger that those born into the community might abandon its most dearly held characteristics (Deut 13). Ezekiel recognizes a similar porousness in Israel's ethnic boundaries, insisting that those who claim Israelite heritage but fail to follow Yhwh will be rejected (Ezek 8–11; 14).

These other texts envision such fluidity largely around the edges of the community. Isaiah 66 – bookended by Isa 56 – takes the possibility that foreigners will hear of and commit themselves to Yhwh to the most extreme conclusion. The present continuous verb – 'the new heavens and the new earth, which *I am making*' (66:22) – to describe Yhwh's new creation signals that the transformation of the existing creation into a new creation is already taking place – it will not be delayed until the eschaton, nor has it already occurred. The ordination of the people as priests and Levites and the affirmation that 'all humanity will come and worship me' (66:23) signals the active involvement of the people in this process.

These final chapters of the book of Isaiah revolve around a vision of Yhwh as the Lord of Creation and the implications of this fact's full recognition. Before the exile, some Israelites had recognized Yhwh as the only God appropriate for them to worship (although the pervasive admonishments to this effect suggest that it was not universally acknowledged). With the destruction of Jerusalem and the displacement of its inhabitants – some taken forcibly to Babylonia, some fleeing to the Transjordan or to Egypt, others forced to migrate within Judah's borders to survive – the people were scattered across the face of the earth. On this magnified international stage, replete with hundreds of competing deities, the Israelites were obliged to reckon with the power and reach of YHWH. The poetry of Second Isaiah reflected a recognition of YHWH's role as Creator of the entire universe: YHWH's power extended not merely to the Israelites and to their small kingdoms in the eastern Mediterranean, but over all of the nations inhabiting the earth. Third Isaiah takes this theological revelation and expounds on its implications. YHWH's invitation to membership in the community of YHWH's chosen people is far more open than anyone had hitherto imagined: foreigners believed to be barred from YHWH's innermost sanctuary are welcomed, and those whose physical limitations had been thought to exclude them from temple service are called to serve.

YHWH's responsibility for all of creation engenders an imperative among YHWH's people to care for all of YHWH's creatures: the homeless, the hungry, the poor, the neglected – all those who are marginalized by discrimination and miscarriages of justice. To serve YHWH means to serve all whom YHWH is gathering into the kingdom, pursuing lives of justice and righteousness that reflect YHWH's own character. Indeed, the new creation will not come about without human participation; humanity is called to orientate its every action towards YHWH and towards the care of YHWH's creation.

Despite its composite nature, this anonymous poetry collectively offers a powerful vision of God's radical inclusivity, as it urges its audience to invite the homeless, the disabled, the poor and the migrant into the Yahwistic community on equal terms with those whose inclusion is hereditary. The beauty of the poetry and imagery of these late Isaianic authors has long been recognized, and continues to inspire people.

At the same time, the force of their conviction and the rancour of their times also elicited a rage for vengeance that helped to inspire later visions of hell. In a twist of justice, only those who fail to follow YHWH's vision of a new creation characterized by radical inclusivity will be excluded from it. The book closes with an image of looking out over a field of rotting corpses of 'the people who have rebelled' against YHWH: 'their worm shall not die, their fire shall not be quenched, and they shall be an abhorrence to all flesh' (66:24; compare 66:15–16). The end of Isaiah, therefore, sets heaven and hell side by side (65:17–25; compare Rev 21).

The authors of Third Isaiah were also the final editors of the book as a whole. They were influenced by the earlier Isaianic tensions between judgement and grace, brought them into focus, and pressed them farther. From the earliest oracles about royal Zion to the latest ones about the new Jerusalem, Isaianic authors consistently expanded their audience's perceptions about the scope of God's involvement in human affairs – until it comprehended everything, though it 'be deep as Sheol or high as heaven' (7:10). Perhaps more than any other biblical authors, the authors of the book of Isaiah transformed the story of a minor city and tiny nation into a microcosm of a divine plan for the entire world. The power, ambition and influence of the Hebrew Bible as a whole owes much to the book of Isaiah.

Further reading

Berges, Ulrich. *The Book of Isaiah: Its Composition and Final Form*. Translated by Millard Lind. Sheffield: Sheffield Phoenix Press, 2012.

Blenkinsopp, Joseph. 'The "Servants of the Lord" in Third Isaiah: Profile of a Pietistic Group in the Persian Epoch.' Pages 392–412 in *'The Place Is Too Small for Us': The Israelite Prophets in Recent Scholarship*. Ed. Robert P. Gordon. Winona Lake, IN: Eisenbrauns, 1995.

Gray, Mark. *Rhetoric and Social Justice in Isaiah*. London: T&T Clark, 2006.

Irudayaraj, Dominic S. *Violence, Otherness and Identity in Isaiah 63: 1–6: The Trampling One Coming from Edom*. London: Bloomsbury, 2017.

Nurmela, Risto. *The Mouth of the Lord Has Spoken: Inner-biblical Allusions in Second and Third Isaiah*. Lanham, MD: Rowman & Littlefield, 2006.

Stromberg, Jacob. *Isaiah after Exile: The Author of Third Isaiah as Reader and Redactor of the Book*. Oxford Theological Monographs. Oxford: Oxford University Press, 2011.

Tiemeyer, Lena-Sofia, and Hans M. Barstad, eds. *Continuity and Discontinuity: Chronological and Thematic Development in Isaiah 40–66*. Göttingen: Vandenhoeck & Ruprecht, 2014.

Further reading

Historical orientation

Kuhrt, Amélie. *The Ancient Near East, c. 3000–330 BC*. 2 vols. London: Routledge, 1997.

Miller, J. Maxwell, and John H. Hayes. *A History of Ancient Israel and Judah*. 2nd ed. Louisville, Ky.: Westminster John Knox, 2006.

Van de Mieroop, Marc. *A History of the Ancient Near East ca. 3000–323 BC*. 3rd edn. Oxford: Wiley Blackwell, 2016.

Other introductory works

Berges, Ulrich. *The Book of Isaiah: Its Composition and Final Form*. Translated by Millard Lind. Hebrew Bible Monographs, 46. Sheffield: Sheffield Phoenix Press, 2012.

Goldingay, John. *The Theology of the Book of Isaiah*. Downers Grove, IL: InterVarsity, 2014.

Sawyer, John F. A. *The Fifth Gospel: Isaiah in the History of Christianity*. New York: Cambridge University Press, 1996.

Stromberg, Jake. *An Introduction to the Study of Isaiah*. London: T&T Clark, 2011.

Stulman, Louis, and Hyun Chul Paul Kim. *You Are My People: An Introduction to Prophetic Literature*. Nashville: Abingdon, 2010.

Tiemeyer, Lena-Sofia, ed. *The Oxford Handbook of Isaiah*. Oxford: Oxford University Press, 2021.

Williamson, H. G. M. *Variations on a Theme: King, Messiah and Servant in the Book of Isaiah*. Carlisle, Cumbria: Paternoster, 1998.

Commentaries

Blenkinsopp, Joseph. *Isaiah: A New Translation with Introduction and Commentary*. Anchor Bible 19. 3 vols. New York: Doubleday, 2000–2003.

Childs, Brevard. *Isaiah*. Old Testament Library. Louisville, KY: Westminster John Knox, 2001.

Hanson, Paul D. *Isaiah 40–66*. Interpretation. Louisville, KY: John Knox, 1995.

Kim, Hyun Chul Paul. *Reading Isaiah: A Literary and Theological Commentary*. Macon, GA: Smyth & Helwys, 2016.

Miscall, Peter D. *Isaiah*. Readings: A New Biblical Commentary. Sheffield: Sheffield Academic, 1993.

Roberts, J. J. M. *First Isaiah: A Commentary*. Hermeneia. Minneapolis, MN: Fortress, 2015.

Sawyer, John F. A. *Isaiah through the Centuries*. Blackwell Bible Commentaries. Oxford: Wiley Blackwell, 2017.

Seitz, Christopher R. *Isaiah 1–39*. Interpretation. Louisville, KY: John Knox, 1993.

Sweeney, Marvin A. *Isaiah*. Forms of Old Testament Literature 16, 19. Grand Rapids, MI: Eerdmans, 1996, 2016.

Tull, Patricia K. *Isaiah 1–39*. Macon, GA: Smyth & Helwys, 2010.

Wildberger, Hans. *Isaiah 1–39*. 3 vols. Continental Commentaries. Minneapolis, MN: Fortress, 1991.

Williams, Jenni. *The Kingdom of Our God: A Theological Commentary on Isaiah*. London: SCM, 2019.

Shorter commentaries

Couey, J. Blake. 'Isaiah, Jeremiah, Ezekiel, Daniel and the Twelve'. Pages 215–73 in *The Bible and Disability: A Commentary*. Ed. Sarah J. Melcher, Mikeal C. Parsons and Amos Yong. Waco, TX: Baylor University Press, 2017.

Fischer, Irmtraud. 'Isaiah: The Book of Female Metaphors'. Pages 303–18 in *Feminist Biblical Interpretation: A Compendium of Critical Commentary on the Boks of the Bible and Related Literature*. Ed. Luise Schottroff and Marie-Theres Wacker. Grand Rapids, MI: Eerdmans, 2012.

Franke, Chris. 'Isaiah 40–66'. Pages 699–724 in *Fortress Commentary on the Bible: The Old Testament and Apocrypha*. Ed. Gale A. Yee, Hugh R. Page Jr. and Matthew J. M. Coomber. Minneapolis, MN: Fortress, 2014.

Premnath, D. N. 'The Empire and First Isaiah'. Pages 240–57 in *Postcolonial Commentary and the Old Testament*. Ed. Hemchand Gossai. London: Bloomsbury, 2019.

Sweeney, Marvin A. 'Isaiah 1–39'. Pages 673–97 in *Fortress Commentary on the Bible: The Old Testament and Apocrypha*. Ed. Gale A. Yee, Hugh R. Page Jr. and Matthew J. M. Coomber. Minneapolis, MN: Fortress, 2014.

Tull, Patricia K. 'Isaiah'. Pages 255–66 in *Women's Bible Commentary*. 3rd edn. Revised and updated. Ed. Carol A. Newsom, Sharon H. Ringe and Jacqueline E. Lapsley. Louisville, KY: Westminster John Knox, 2012.

Timeline

In the early first millennium (1000–800 BCE), the ancient Near East was still emerging from the international political vacuum caused by the collapse of Late Bronze Age powers. Egypt and Assyria were both caught up in affairs close to home, and did not have the resources to rule the southern Levant.

In the absence of a strong imperial power, a number of small kingdoms sprang up in the Levant, including Israel, Judah, Moab, Aram and Philistia. Without the burden of an imperial overlord or tribute payments, many of these experienced a period of relative prosperity, especially in the eighth century. Isaiah ben Amoz began to prophesy in the late eighth century, when Mesopotamian imperialism began to be felt again.

750

745: Tiglath-pileser III becomes king in Assyria and begins westward expansion.

734–731: The 'Syro-Ephraimite' crisis, in which Israel and Aramean city-states waged war on Judah to try to unite the Levant in resisting Assyria (2 Kgs 16:5–9).

721: Israel withholds tribute from Assyria (2 Kgs 17:4), prompting Sargon II to besiege Samaria. The city is defeated and much of its population deported. Israel is broken up into Assyrian provinces. Deportees from elsewhere in the empire are brought to repopulate the region.

705: Sargon II dies and Judah rebels, led by King Hezekiah.

701: The new Assyrian king, Sennacherib, attacks Judah and gains its resubmission, but does not destroy Jerusalem (2 Kgs 18:14–16).

700

Seventh century: Judah, under Hezekiah and Manasseh, submits to the Assyrian empire, but is not turned into a province.

650

621(?): Josiah enacts religious and political reforms in Jerusalem (2 Kgs 22–23). Assyrian power begins to weaken; rebellions break out across the empire.

612: Babylonia succeeds Assyria as the dominant power in Mesopotamia. Babylonia and Egypt fight for control of the Levant; Judah vacillates between the two.

600 — 597: Judah rebels while a Babylonia vassal; Nebuchadnezzar lays
siege to Jerusalem and defeats it, deporting the royal family
and the king (Jehoiachin) to Babylon and installing Zedekiah as
king (2 Kgs 24:10–17).

587: Judah rebels again; Nebuchadnezzar besieges Jerusalem
for a second time, destroys the city, and orders further
deportations (2 Kgs 24:20–25:11).

586–536: Many Judean elites taken to Exile in Babylonia; part of
population remains in Judah; Jerusalem and the Temple are
not rebuilt.

550 —

539: The Persians, led by Cyrus, defeats the Babylonians and take
over and expand their empire.

536: The Edict of Cyrus allows Judeans and their descendants to
return to their homelands (Ezra 1); Judah is part of a Persian
province.

515(?): Rebuilding of the temple in Jerusalem, perhaps with Persian
support.

500 —

Fifth century: Missions of Ezra and Nehemiah from Babylonia to
Jerusalem; regular correspondence between Jerusalem
temple leadership and Egyptian diaspora communities such
as Elephantine; increasing evidence of sectarian disputes
within the community.

Index of subjects

Index of biblical references